P9-BBV-446

Making
Classic Wreaths

Making
Classic Wreaths

DESIGNING & CREATING FOR ALL SEASONS

Ed Smith

Sterling Publishing Co., Inc.

New York

Prolific Impressions Production Staff:

Editor in Chief: Mickey Baskett
Copy Editor: Phyllis Mueller
Graphics: Dianne Miller, Karen Turpin
Styling: Lenos Key
Photography: Jerry Mucklow
Administration: Jim Baskett

Every effort has been made to insure that the information presented is accurate. Since we have no control over physical conditions, individual skills, or chosen tools and products, the publisher disclaims any liability for injuries, losses, untoward results, or any other damages which may result from the use of the information in this book. Thoroughly read the instructions for all products used to complete the projects in this book, paying particular attention to all cautions and warnings shown for that product to ensure their proper and safe use.

No part of this book may be reproduced for commercial purposes in any form without permission by the copyright holder. The written instructions and design patterns in this book are intended for the personal use of the reader and may be reproduced for that purpose only.

Library of Congress Cataloging-in-Publication Data Available

10 9 8 7 6 5 4 3 2

Published by Sterling Publishing Co., Inc.
387 Park Avenue South, New York, N.Y. 10016

© 2004 by Prolific Impressions, Inc.

Produced by Prolific Impressions, Inc.
160 South Candler St., Decatur, GA 30030

Distributed in Canada by Sterling Publishing
c/o Manda Group, 165 Dufferin Street
Toronto, Ontario, Canada M6K 3H6
Distributed in Great Britain by Chrysalis Books Group PLC,
The Chrysalis Building, Bramley Road, London W10 6SP, England
Distributed in Australia by Capricorn Link (Australia) Pty. Ltd.
P.O. Box 704, Windsor, NSW 2756 Australia

Printed in China
All rights reserved
Sterling ISBN 1-4027-1408-4

For information about custom editions, special sales, premium and corporate purchases, please contact Sterling Special Sales Department at 800-805-5489 or specialsales@sterlingpub.com

ACKNOWLEDGEMENTS

I would like to thank the following manufacturers for their generosity in supplying materials for this book.

For pan melt glue and floral spray paints:
Floralife, Inc., 751 Thunderbolt Drive, Walterboro, SC 29488, 800-323-3689, www.floralife.com

For ribbons:
Berwick Offray LLC, Rt. 24, Box 601, Chester, NJ 07930, 800-327-0350, www.offray.com

For Styrofoam® wreaths, extruded foam wreaths, and chenille stems:
Styrofoam-Chenille, P.O. Box 252, Ludington, MI 49431, 231-843-6580, www.Styrofoam-chenille.com
Styrofoam® is a registered trademark of Dow Chemical.

For glitter spray, spray adhesives, clear sprays, and spray paints:
Krylon Products Group, Cleveland, OH 44115, 800-797-3332, www.krylon.com

For craft glues:
Beacon Adhesives Company, Inc., 125 South MacQuesten Parkway, Mount Vernon, NY 10550, 914-699-3400, www.beaconadhesives.com

For dried lavender:
The Cutting Garden, 303 Dahlia Llama Lane, Sequim, Washington 98382, 360-681-3099, www.cuttinggarden.com

For floral spray paints:
Design Master, P.O. Box 601, Boulder, CO 80306, 303-443-5214, www.dmcolor.com

About the Author

Ed Smith has always been passionate about creating. He graduated from Ball State University with a B.S. and an M.A. in art education, taught art in elementary and high schools, and has been active in developing and teaching design classes for adults.

For several years, Ed owned a company that designed and manufactured handcrafted gifts for the wholesale market. Today he divides his time, working as a freelance florist, artist, and designer. Over 200 of his designs have been published in magazines, on websites, and as project sheets, and he is the author of *Wall Flowers for All Seasons*, 2003 by Grace Publications.

Ed is a member of the American Institute of Floral Designers and the Society of Craft Designers. His enthusiasm, talent, and creativity have made him a sought-after designer and teacher. You can contact Ed and see more of his work on his website, www.edsmithdesigns.com.

Thank You

All great wreaths begin with great products, and I thank the generous manufacturers that provided supplies: Floralife, for pot melt glue and floral sprays, Offray for ribbon, Dow and Florcraft for Styrofoam® and straw wreaths, Beacon Adhesives for glue, and Krylon for spray paints and spray glitter.

Thanks to my family and friends who encouraged me in making this book a reality. A huge thank you to all the people who have said, "I like that wreath" - your support and friendships inspire me to continue the creative process.

C O N T

Simple Circles

I have always been fascinated and delighted with wreaths. Seeing a wreath on the front door or centered over a mantel says welcome and brings a smile to my face. Maybe it is their simple universal shape, or perhaps it is the infinite possibilities of design. Whatever the reason, I love to design and create wreaths. As a professional florist and designer, I have made hundreds of wreaths - some elaborate and showy, others plain and simple - each with its own unique personality. Each time I begin a wreath I am excited to explore all the creative possibilities of a simple circle.

In this book I'll show you how to make a wide variety of wreaths and teach you techniques that yield great results. Knowing a few simple tips and tricks will help you create professional, beautifully crafted wreaths. You will use many of the tips over and over as you create your wreaths.

You will first learn the basics - what tools and materials you need to successfully and efficiently create your wreaths. Learn what wreath bases are required for the various types of materials you are using to make the wreaths. Step by step photos will show you techniques required for the types of wreath designs featured. I will not only show you how to create with silk and dried flowers, but I also give tips for using fresh greenery and fresh flowers in your designs.

Take your time and choose quality materials to ensure a beautiful, long-lasting wreath. I encourage you to make substitutions and explore your own creative ideas as you work. Let your wreaths **express your personality**, and feel free to use the projects and supplies lists as guidelines rather than rules. Let the projects in this book inspire you to make some classic wreaths of your own.

Beginning a wreath, adding the design elements, and admiring the finished design are all fun steps in the process of crafting wreaths. My most important tips are have fun, use your creative ideas, and let your materials guide you in crafting wreaths you will be proud to say you made.

Wreath History

Wreaths have a rich history. They were first made in ancient Persia and worn around the head on religious occasions. These wreaths were *diadem,* from a Greek word meaning "bound around." A diadem was a symbol of royalty or spiritual significance, and many cultures adopted the diadem. Ancient Romans used wreaths as headpieces to denote royalty or status and to celebrate festive occasions, and in 776 B.C., they began crowning victors of athletic competitions with laurel leaf wreaths.

No one is sure how the wreath went from the head to the wall, but it is speculated that a laurel leaf wreath was hung on a wall after a celebration. Before long wreath makers were assigning spiritual purposes to their creations. A holly wreath was believed to shelter a home from the cold spirits of winter. A young woman who presented a man with a wreath made of birch twigs indicated she was interested in him as a lover.

Today's wreaths continue to reflect the spirit of the maker. They still are used at important life occasions, including the celebration of love and holidays and the death of a loved one.

Floral Crafting Tools & Supplies

Before you begin to make wreaths, you will need to assemble some basic tools and supplies to make each step easy and professional. Most items are available at craft stores and stores that sell florist's supplies.

CUTTING & MEASURING TOOLS

• **Wire Cutters**

(#1 in photo)

Wire cutters are used in almost every design so choose a well-constructed pair with easy to grip handles. A good pair can make your wreaths a breeze to complete, while an inferior pair is painful for your hands. Choose a pair with a spring in the handle and blades that open wide enough to accommodate most silk flower stems - wire cutters are an important tool when working with silk flowers.

• **Bolt Cutters**

(#2)

Bolt cutters make it easy to cut heavy stems. Find them at hardware stores.

• **Pruning Shears**

(#3)

Pruning shears are the perfect tool for cutting vines, branches, and twigs. (You can cut natural materials with wire cutters, but pruning shears will make a cleaner, smoother cut.)

• **Knives**

(#4)

A good quality, sharp knife is a must for cutting natural stems - cut fresh stems at a 45-degree angle to allow them to draw water easily.

A household knife with a serrated edge works well for cutting and shaping foam. To make cutting foam easier and faster, run the knife blade across an old candle or a bar of soap.

• **Scissors**

(#5)

I recommend having two pairs of scissors - one for general cutting and one for ribbon. Use the general ones for paper and ribbon with a wire edge and the other for plain-edge ribbon and fabric. Don't use scissors to cut floral wire; the wire will quickly dull and damage your scissors.

• **Other Useful Tools**

Tape measure or ruler, for measuring (#6)
Pencil, for marking
Small hammer, for helping insert floral U-pins (#7)
Gloves to protect your hands

#7

#6

#3

#5

#4

#1

#2

SUPPLIES FOR ATTACHING ITEMS TO WREATHS

• Wired Wood Picks

(#1 in photo)

Wood picks are small pointed wood sticks with an attached wire that are used to lengthen stems, provide support, and bind items together. Wood picks come in a variety of sizes (common lengths are 2", 3" and 6") and colors (brown, natural, green).

Picks make it easier to insert items such as small clusters of flowers, ribbon loops, and bows in a wreath. The pick's sharp point gives a tight, twist-resistant insertion. Wood picks inserted in wet floral foam will expand from the moisture and increase their holding power. Items attached to a wood pick can be covered with floral tape for added security and to camouflage the wire.

• Wood Skewers

(#2)

Wood skewers are ideal for securing fresh or artificial fruits and vegetables in a wreath - simply insert the sharp end. Use natural wood skewers for fresh items - dyed ones discolor fresh fruits and vegetables and make them unfit for eating.

• Cable Ties

(#3)

Cable ties - the kind commonly used to bundle electrical wires, cords, and cables - are wonderfully useful in wreath crafting. They can securely hold stems, vines, and branches that would be difficult to do with wire alone. Cable tie are sold in many lengths and colors. They can be purchased at home improvement, hardware, and office supply stores.

• Chenille Stems

(#4)

Chenille stems (sometimes called *pipe cleaners*) are an easy, secure way to create a hanging loop for many kinds of wreaths. They come in a variety of colors. Metallic and brightly colored chenille stems are fun to twist and curl as accents in wreaths.

For a hanging loop, choose a chenille stem that will blend into your wreath, like moss green or brown. A couple of chenille stems can be twisted together to hang heavier wreaths, and they can be further secured with glue and floral U-pins. The soft fiber of the chenille stem helps it grip, and it won't scratch surfaces like floral wire might.

• Floral Tape

(#5)

Floral tape is a self-sealing, colorfast, waterproof wrap that stretches to cover and camouflage wires, stems, and picks. Floral tape is not adhesive - it sticks to itself when stretched. The slightly sticky texture of the tape helps hold wires and other materials in place. It comes in a variety of widths and colors, including several shades of green, brown, black, and white. Choose a floral tape that blends with your design, such as brown on a natural twig or green on a stem.

• Floral U-Pins

(#6)

Floral U-pins, which are sometimes referred to as *greening pins*, are U-shaped wires that can secure materials like stems, moss, and ribbon to a wreath. They're easy to use - simply place an item on a wreath base and insert the pin, or secure flower stems with U-pins by placing the stem under the pin. For the best grip, insert a couple of pins at 45-degree angles in opposite directions. U-pins are most secure if you dip them in glue before inserting.

• Floral Wire

(#7)

Floral wire comes in many gauges (thicknesses) and lengths. The higher the gauge, the thinner and more flexible the wire. Heavy gauge wire, like 16 gauge, would be used for strengthening a heavy stem and providing support. Lighter gauge wire, like 22, is great for making bows and binding stems together.

Floral wire can be green or galvanized; green is most often used. **It is sold in straight lengths or on a spool as paddle wire.** Floral wire on a paddle is useful for making garlands and for binding or securing items to a wreath.

• Straight Pins

(#8)

Straight pins are useful for securing items like ribbon to wreaths and can be used to hold items in place.

• Sandpaper

(#9)

Used most often to smooth and shape plastic foam wreaths. It can also be used to removed rust from wire.

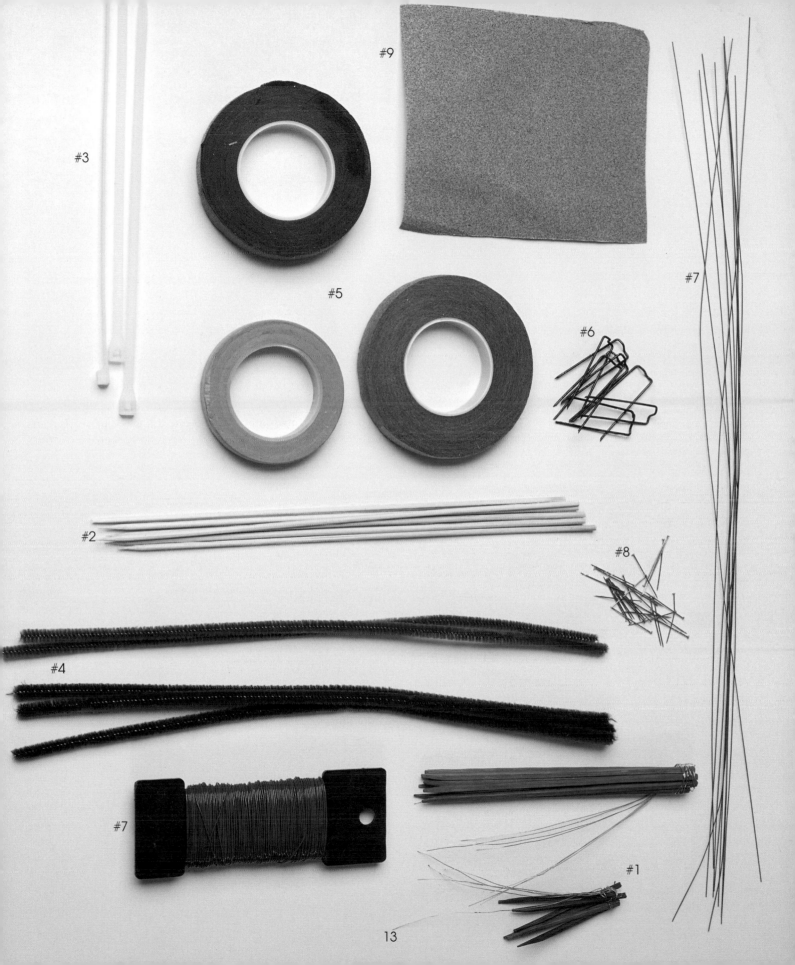

#9

#3

#5

#6

#7

#2

#8

#4

#7

#1

13

GLUES

• Glue Guns

Glue guns come in several types - low temperature and high temperature are the most common. A *high temperature glue gun* can be used for most floral projects, and the glue creates a strong, fast bond. Use it to easily glue silk flowers, dried materials, and novelty items to a wreath. A *low temperature glue gun* is best for use on Styrofoam® and other materials that are heat sensitive.

TIP: Keep a bowl of cool water close at hand as you work with a glue gun. If you get any hot glue on your hand, quickly dip your hand in the water to help prevent a serious burn.

• White Craft Glue

Heavy-bodied white craft glues are a great way to adhere some floral items. White glue dries more slowly than hot glue, allowing you more time to adjust items before the glue sets up. White craft glue is great for covering large surfaces (like a foam wreath with potpourri). It is also excellent for adhering ribbon trims where a glue gun may leave a bumpy surface or stain the ribbon.

• Clear Glues

Industrial strength clear glues are great for attaching heavier objects to your wreaths. This type of glue is also good when gluing non-porous items such as glass and metal.

• Hot Melt Pan Glue

This glue, which is similar to hot glue sticks, is melted in an electric skillet to a creamy consistency. Pan melt glue comes in pellets and chunks. The advantage of pan melt glue is that it's easy to dip items in the glue and insert them in your wreath. Pan melt glue typically is as strong and flexible as other types of glue.

PAINTS

• Floral Spray Paints

Floral spray paints can add a touch of color or change colors in a design easily. Typically, they are translucent and lightly color flowers and accessories. They are safe for fresh flowers as well as silk and dried ones, and they can be used on Styrofoam® because they won't dissolve it as some solvent-based paints will. I often use wood-tone sprays to add a fresh look to faded grapevine wreaths or to tone down and antique colors that are a bit too bright.

• Sealers

Clear spray sealers in matte and gloss finish can be used to spray dried materials to keep them from shattering. (A couple of thin coats will produce the best results.) Spraying items in a cardboard box contains the overspray and makes cleanup easy.

• Special Effects Sprays

There are a variety of spray mediums that will result in interesting effects - such as glitter sprays, leaf-fresh sprays, frosting sprays, etc.

• Acrylic Craft Paint

Acrylic craft paint can be used to paint foam wreaths or to add color to natural materials. It comes in a huge variety of pre-mixed colors and cleanup is easy - just use soap and water. Apply craft paint with a 1" **foam brush** or **artist brush.**

STEMMING MACHINE

Optional

A stemming machine attaches a sharp metal pick to floral stems, allowing for easy, secure insertion of stems in floral foam, dry foam, or Styrofoam®. Picks can be 1-3/4", 2-1/8", or 3" long. A stemming machine is an investment and a wonderful tool for people who want to produce quantities of floral wreaths.

Wreath Bases

All wreaths have one common denominator - a base. Choices of bases are wide and varied - straw, grapevine, plastic foam (Styrofoam®), and wire are some examples. Even if your base is completely covered, choosing the right base will make designing easier and the results professional-looking.

When choosing a base, consider the materials you will be using. Are they heavy? Delicate? How will they be attached? Where the wreath will hang can also help you choose the right base. Each wreath base has a specific purpose. Projects in this book use a variety of bases, allowing you to see the differences in their performance. Wreath base descriptions and their characteristics follow.

Straw

Straw wreaths are inexpensive and are manufactured in a wide variety of sizes, from 6" to 36". The straw is tightly wrapped in nylon string to form a compact, sturdy base. Materials can be attached with glue, U-pins, picks, or wire. Straw is attractive enough to leave exposed; its texture and color can be part of the design. Because straw bases are chunky, it is difficult to make thin, airy wreaths on a straw base. Straw wreaths are good for both indoor and outdoor display, and they can be used again and again if the floral materials are inserted or wired on the wreath rather than glued.

Straw wreaths are sometimes sold wrapped in clear or green plastic. You can either leave on the plastic wrap or remove it, depending on the type of wreath you are creating; if you are completely covering the wreath, you may prefer to leave it wrapped.

Straw

Plastic Foam (Styrofoam®)

Plastic foam wreath bases come in green and white; and in a variety of sizes and special shapes like hearts and stars with straight or beveled edges. They are lightweight and easy to cut and shape, and they can be easily painted with acrylic paints or sprayed with paints that are safe for use on plastic foam. (Use caution - some paints and solvents will dissolve plastic foam.) This material will not absorb water or attract insects so it is great for use outdoors.

Because of its firm structure, plastic foam tightly grips floral materials. Materials can be glued, attached with floral U-pins, and inserted directly. Styrofoam wreaths are not suitable for lots of heavy insertions because of their tendency to break. To strengthen a plastic foam wreath, I often glue on a cardboard backing.

Plastic foam

Extruded Foam

Extruded foam wreaths are rounded, have a smooth appearance, and are often confused with plastic foam wreaths. Extruded foam wreaths are available in green and white, often supported inside with a wire ring.

Because of their smooth texture they are ideal for painting or gluing - materials like seeds, leaves, and flower petals can easily be glued to extruded wreaths. Picks and floral U-pins can be used with extruded wreaths.

Extruded Foam

Wire

Wire frame wreath bases are available in a wide variety of sizes in both single wire and box styles. Materials like dried flowers, fresh greens, and pinecones can be attached to them with paddle wire. Wire wreath bases are light and sturdy so they can be used with both heavy and light materials. (Dried materials are great to use on wire wreath bases.)

Because many items cannot be directly inserted into a wire frame, a wreath with a wire base often takes more time to complete; however, the results are worth the effort. You can make a quick wreath by simply wiring a purchased garland to a wire wreath base.

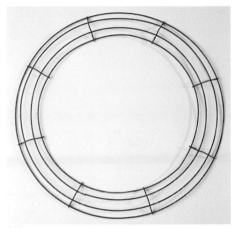

Wire

Natural Vine

The most common natural wreaths are made from grapevines and honeysuckle vines. These wreaths are sold in an endless variety of shapes and sizes. Curly willow, birch twigs, and other natural materials are also fashioned into wreath bases that can vary from thick and chunky to light and airy.

Floral materials can be attached to natural wreaths with glue, wire, picks, and floral U-pins. The wreath bases can be completely covered or left partly exposed, giving you a grand variety of style options. Natural wreath bases can be used over and over by simply removing the old floral materials and adding new ones.

Natural vine

Wood

Circles of wood or pressed fiberboard can provide a sturdy base for heavy and hard-to-attach items. Rocks, seashells, and nuts can all be glued to them. Wooden wreath bases are available in craft stores, or you can cut them yourself from plywood using a jigsaw.

Floral Foam

Wreath forms made of floral foam are meant to be used with freshly cut flowers. The wreath base is soaked in water and the flowers are inserted directly in the foam. Flowers like roses and hydrangeas can be inserted in the moist foam and allowed to dry in place. Floral foam wreath bases are backed with plastic for support.

Ready-to-Decorate Bases

If you're in a hurry, consider ready-made wreath bases - wreaths made of lemon leaves, eucalyptus, grasses, baby's breath, pine boughs, and many more are available ready made. Simply add embellishments like flowers and ribbon. When choosing a natural dried wreath, check to be sure there is not excessive shedding. Artificial pine and cedar wreath bases are a fast way to start a wreath and economical as well.

Flowers & Foliage

Flower Types

Filler

Line

Filler

Line

Form

Mass

Choosing Silk Flowers

"Silk flowers" is the loose term for almost any artificial flower, whether the flower is made of fabric, paper, latex, or plastic. Selecting quality silk flowers will enhance your finished wreath and make designing easier. Here are some guidelines and tips:

- Choose flowers with *good attention to detail.* Look for veins, stamen, and subtle color variations.
- Flowers that are *natural in color* are always a good choice. Although many silk flowers are manufactured in exactly the same color, try to select a variety of color variations for a more realistic look.
- Look for flowers with *wire inside the blossoms and leaves* so they can be shaped easily. Take time to shape the flowers as you work - starting at the base of the stem, shape the leaves and blossoms and bend the stems into gentle curves for a natural-looking appearance.
- Quality silk flowers will have *blossoms that are securely attached* to the stem. Open some blossoms (if possible) to achieve different sizes, texture, and visual interest.
- Don't be afraid to *prune foliage stems* to remove some leaves and create a more natural look.
- Rejuvenate the *frayed edges* on silk flowers and leaves by trimming them with scissors. Flowers with badly frayed edges can be held near a heat gun to seal the edges.

Choosing Fresh Flowers

Fresh flowers are a delightful way to enhance almost any wreath. Although the wreaths here all use dried and silk flowers, fresh cut flowers can be substituted easily in some designs. The beauty of fresh blossoms can enhance a wreath made for a special day or celebration. Of course a fresh wreath will not last as long as a silk or dried wreath but the extra effort and special "in-the-moment" quality of fresh wreaths make them wonderful works of art.

When using fresh flowers choose blossoms that are in their prime or beginning to fully open. Prepare the flowers by cutting the stems at an angle and placing them in water with a floral preservative added. Remove any foliage that will be below the water to prevent any decay or rapid growth of bacteria. Be sure the flowers are well hydrated before arranging into the wreath. Allowing the flowers to stand in water for at least a few hours will help extend their beauty in the wreath.

In many of the designs where flowers are inserted into plastic foam (Styrofoam®), fresh floral foam can be substituted. Fresh floral foam should be soaked in water until it is fully hydrated. Fill a sink or deep container with water and place the foam into the water and allow it to fully absorb the water. Do not hold the foam under the water as this may cause the foam to not fully absorb leaving dry places in the foam. Fully hydrated foam will float slightly above the water. If possible use a commercially available floral preservative added to the water to extend the life of the cut flowers. After the fresh foam is fully soaked, cut it to the needed size with a knife.

Wrapping the moist foam in thin plastic or foil will help it retain its moisture. When designing, simply poke the flower stems thru the plastic or foil or use a knife to make a hole and insert the flowers. Be sure you insert your flowers deeply into the foam. Deep insertions will keep the flowers secure and allow for the flowers to drink in more moisture. The wrapped foam can be taped to the wreath with adhesive tape or held in place with chenille stems. Generally I like to insert my fresh flowers first, followed by any foliage. After completing your wreath, allow it to hang in a place where water will not damage anything if it drips from the foam.

Wedding bouquet holders and other plastic forms with attached fresh foam can also be used with success in wreaths. Simply cut the handles of a bouquet holder to a short length. After you have soaked it, glue it to the wreath.

Instead of using floral foam, some types of flowers can simply be inserted into a grapevine wreath or wired onto a wire frame base. Hydrangeas, and filler flowers like babies breathe and statice all work beautifully using this technique. These flowers look beautiful when fresh and then will dry in place for a long lasting design.

Flower Types

See page 18 for example.

Shopping for flowers can seem almost overwhelming. Step into any floral supply or craft store and you will find hundreds of choices. To help you select flowers for your wreaths, I have divided them into categories that describe their general shape and appearance. Project instructions in the book suggest specific flowers, but you can **substitute a similar flower** in the same category (e.g., one line flower for another line flower) if you want a different color or the flower specified isn't available.

Line Flowers

Line flowers are blossoms that grow in a linear shape. Line flowers help establish the height and width of a design, and they often create movement and direction in a wreath. Line flowers include snapdragon, gladiolus, delphinium, larkspur, and liatris. Grasses, twigs, and long, slender leaves can be used to create similar effects.

Form Flowers

Form flowers have distinctive shapes that are the same on each flower. The distinct shapes of the blossoms make this flower type ideal for creating the focal point in your wreath. Form flowers include the calla lily, tulip, iris, bird of paradise, and lily.

Mass Flowers

Mass flowers have large numbers of blossoms or small clusters of blossoms at the end of a stem. Mass flowers are used to create both focal points and volume in a design. Mass flowers include the hydrangea, peony, carnation, open rose, and large mum.

Filler Flowers

Filler flowers are multi-stemmed flowers that often have branching shapes. They fill in space and add depth and texture to a design. Filler flowers include statice, baby's breath, and small field flowers.

Foliage & Accents

How you use foliage and accents in your wreaths makes the difference between "okay" and "great." Foliage can add great dimension, color, texture, and movement to wreaths - it is the background (and often the unifying element) of a wreath.

When choosing foliage, keep in mind the look you want to achieve; for example, are you creating texture or adding height? Often the addition of a beautiful foliage or berry spray ties a design together for a polished, professional look.

Using accents like fruits, vegetables, and elements like seashells helps create texture and set a mood.

Pictured above: Life-like fruit is available and makes great accents to a wreath

Pictured left: A variety of foliage and accents are important to your wreath design.

Mosses

Mosses are a wonderful addition to almost any design. They add texture and color while creating a natural feel. Green sheet moss, Spanish moss, and reindeer moss can be used to hide elements like foam, picks, and glue. You can use moss to cover a base before flowers are inserted or glue it on afterwards.

Mosses come preserved and dried. Sheet moss can be soaked in water before using to make it more pliable and help restore some of its fresh green color. I often thin green acrylic craft paint with water, pour it in a spray bottle, and spray it on dried moss to recreate the look of fresh moss.

1 - Sheet Moss

2 - Green-dyed Spanish Moss

3 - Reindeer Moss

4 - Natural Spanish Moss

Basic Techniques

Here are the techniques you need to learn to become successful at wreath-making. Learning the correct way to work with florals is important to the look and longevity of your wreath design.

Using Floral Tape to Lengthen a Stem

1. Working from the roll of tape, unroll a small length. Place the end of the tape on the stem or wire to be covered.

2. Gently stretching the tape toward yourself, roll the tape diagonally, overlapping it to cover the wire. Stretching the tape in long, tight spirals will create a smooth covering. Tear the tape at the end of the wire.

Adding a Wood Pick

A wood pick is added to a stem for strength.

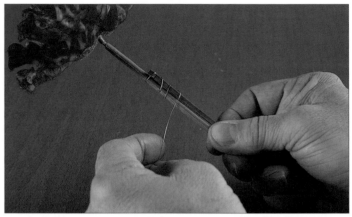

1. Hold the pick parallel to the stem, overlapping about 1". Twist the wire from the pick around the stem and the wood, working down the stem and pick. Make sure the last couple of twists of wire are below the stem and only on the pick.

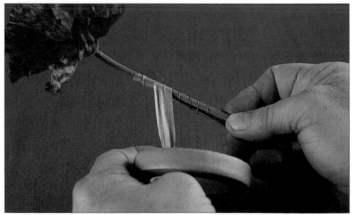

2. Wrap the stem with floral tape to conceal the wire and secure the pick and stem.

Securing Florals to Wreaths with Floral U-Pins

1. Place stem on wreath. Insert the U-pin across the stem at a 45 degree angle.

2. Add a second U-pin in the opposite direction for a tight grip.

Securing Florals Using a Cable Tie

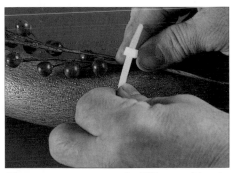

Place stem on wreath. Wrap cable tie around wreath and stem. Slip end through loop and pull to secure. Trim end of tie.

Maintaining Perspective

As you work on your wreath, you'll want to be able to observe your progress and make design decisions based on how the wreath will look when it is displayed. It is difficult to see the proper perspective if you work with it flat on a table. Working with the wreath on an easel or hanging the wreath on a wall as you design will help you achieve the proper perspective. Another option is to lean a long piece of shelving lumber with a nail near the top against your work table - it's a great, inexpensive way to have a work surface with the right perspective.

If you cannot work with your wreath hanging, hang it on a wall periodically as you work to be sure you have a pleasing look.

Hanging Your Wreath

For secure display, it's a good idea for every wreath to have a hanger, made either from a chenille stem or from floral wire wrapped in floral tape. For most designs, it is best to attach the hanger before adding flowers.

After you've attached your hanger, test it to be sure the wreath lies flat when hung. Be sure the hanger is not visible from the front when the wreath is hung.

Two hangers are a good idea on large, heavy, or odd-shaped wreaths. Place the hangers, equally spaced from the top, at each side of the wreath.

Chenille Stem Hanger
Chenille stems make great hangers for most wreaths.
1. Bend a 12" chenille stem into a U-shape.
2. Slip it through or around the wreath or insert it in the wreath.
3. Twist the ends together to secure.

Hangers on a Vine Wreath

1. To attach a hanger to a grapevine wreath, spread the vines by gently inserting a kitchen knife through the vines at the top of the wreath and turning the knife blade to make an opening. Insert the chenille stem through the opening made by the knife. Be sure the chenille stem won't be visible from the front.

2. Twist the ends of the chenille stem together, then twist to make a loop. Adjust as needed.

continued from page 23

Hangers on a Plastic Foam, Extruded Foam, or Straw Wreath

1. Cut chenille stem in half. Attach to a wooden pick.

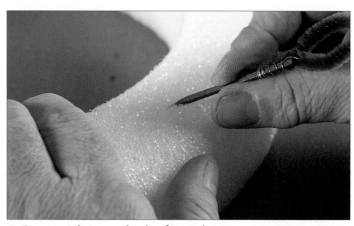

2. Insert pick in top back of wreath.

3. Secure with floral U-pins and glue.

Wrapped Floral Wire Hanger

If a chenille stem is not long enough, use floral wire wrapped in floral tape. The tape helps keep the wire from slipping, and it keeps the wire from scratching a wall or door.
1. Cut a length of wire.
2. Wrap the wire in floral tape as described in the Basic Techniques section.
3. Slip the wrapped wire through or around the wreath or insert it in the wreath.
4. Twist the ends together to secure.

Caring for Wreaths

Proper care will keep your wreath fresh looking and extend its life. Here are some tips:

• To preserve the life of any wreath, keep it out of direct sunlight and away from sources of direct heat like air vents.

• For most silk flower wreaths, an occasional dusting is all that is needed - use a feather duster or a small artist's brush. A hair dryer on low heat can also remove dust. Commercial silk spray cleaners are available - they work well on really dusty wreaths. Read and follow the instructions carefully.

• Dried flowers on wreaths can be perked up with a light coat of clear acrylic spray.

• Bows can be smoothed and refreshed with a curling iron on low heat.

• To store an out-of-season wreath, stuff the loops of bows with tissue paper to help them retain their shape and place the wreath in a dark plastic bag. Hang in a cool, dry location.

• Spray a badly faded or less than beautiful wreath with metallic gold or silver paint for a whole new look.

Design Placement Ideas

For most wreath designs, you'll be creating a focal point and adding flowers and greens around the focal point. Here are some examples of focal point placement:

Wreath totally covered with foliage and/or flowers. (The whole wreath is the focal point.)

Bottom Focal Point Placement: Focal point centered at the bottom of the wreath, accented with foliage and flowers.

Top Focal Point Placement: Focal point centered at the top of the wreath, accented with foliage and flowers.

continued on next page

Continued from page 25

Upper Left: Focal point at about 10 o'clock, accented with foliage and flowers.

Lower right: Focal point at about 4 o'clock, accented with foliage and flowers.

Vertical: Focal point created with a strong vertical line at either the bottom or the top of the wreath.

Horizontal: Focal point created with a strong horizontal line at either the bottom or the top of the wreath.

Ribbons & Bows

Ribbons and bows are a wonderful addition to almost any wreath - the beautiful flowing quality of ribbon creates a sense of movement. Ribbons come unwired and wired; the wired variety has a thin wire running along each edge. Wired ribbons are a good choice if you want the ribbon to maintain a certain shape. Unwired ribbons will give a less structured look and are usually less expensive. It's also fun to use other materials like rope or yarn for bow-making.

Photo 1

Photo 2

Photo 3

Ribbon Rules

- Choose a ribbon that accents or reinforces the theme of your design. For a pretty, delicate wreath, choose a sheer ribbon; for a woodsy wreath, a natural texture might work well.
- Use ribbon as a part of the wreath, incorporating it with the flowers and materials - don't just stick it on.
- If your bow looks like a bow tie, it's probably not the most pleasing use of ribbon.
- Keep scale in mind. The width of the ribbon as well as the size of the bow should be harmonious with the scale of the wreath. Bows that are either to small or too big draw attention to the bow, rather than the overall design.

Graduated Loop Bow

This is an easy-to-make bow with a tailored look. It's best to make it with a ribbon that is the same on both sides.

1. Hold the ribbon between your thumb and index finger, letting the length of ribbon you want as the streamer hang down. Form the smallest loops of the bow, first making one on the left, then making a loop the same size as the first on the right. *Photo 1*

2. Working from the back of the bow, make the next pair of loops slightly larger than the first pair, stacking them on the smaller loops. Continue making pairs of loops left and right, increasing the size of each pair, until the bow is as full as you want it to be. *Photo 2*

3. Place a piece of wire around the front of the bow and take the wire around to the back. Twist the wire at the back of the bow. Leave the ends of the wire long so you can use them to attach the bow to the wreath. *Photo 3*

4. Leave a length of ribbon the same size as the first streamer and trim. Leave the bow as is for a more tailored look or rearrange the loops for a fuller bow. *Photo 4*

Continued on next page

Photo 4

continued from page 27

Florist's Bow

This is the classic, professional-looking bow. To make it, you can use ribbon that is not the same on both sides.

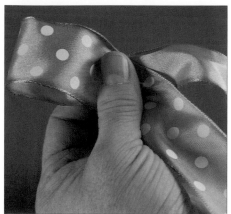

1. Hold the ribbon between your thumb and index finger, letting the length of ribbon you want as the streamer hang down. With the right side of the ribbon facing out, make a loop the size of the largest loop you want on the left. Pinch the ribbon together.

2. Fully twist the ribbon so the right side is facing up.

3. Make the right loop. Make a slightly larger loop to the left under the first set of loops.

4. Continue making loops, working from front to back and alternating left and right, twisting the ribbon so the right side is up and making the loops increasing bigger, until you have made as many loops as you want the bow to have.

5. To finish the bow, twist the ribbon around your thumb to make a small center loop. Cut the end of the second streamer the same as the first.

6. Secure the bow by inserting a piece of floral wire through the center loop, pinching tightly. Pass the ends of the wire to the back and twist tightly. Fan out the loops of the bow. Trim the ribbon ends.

Loopy Bow

This is a full-looking, symmetrical bow. All the loops are the same size.

1. Hold the ribbon between your thumb and index finger, letting the length of ribbon you want as the streamer hang down. Form a loop on the left that is the size you want all the loops to be.

2. Make a loop to the right side the same size as the first. Continue making loops to the left and right until the bow has the desired fullness. Leave a length of ribbon the same size as the first streamer.

3. Put wire across the center of the bow. Turn the bow to the back. Pinch the center of the ribbon and secure the center with the wire. Leave the ends of the wire long so you can use them to attach the bow to the wreath. Fan out the loops of the bow. Trim the ends of the ribbon.

Finishing Ribbon Ends

Use these for plain or wired ribbon.

Diagonal cut.

Dovetail - Fold end in half lengthwise. Cut from the edge to the fold at an angle. Unfold.

Rolled end

This works only for wire-edge ribbon.

Pointed end - Fold ribbon in half lengthwise. Cut from the fold to the edge at a slant. Unfold.

Straight cut.

Designer Tip:

Sometimes the thin wires on wired ribbon stick out beyond the cut ends. To remedy this, gather the ribbon along the wire away from the cut end and trim the wires. Smooth the ribbon back in place.

THE PROJECTS

The following sections of the book show you how to make more than 40 wreaths on a variety of bases. Each project includes photographs, a list of supplies, and instructions for constructing the wreath. I've also estimated the amount of time it would take to make the wreath and the wreath's level of difficulty.

TIME

About an hour

1 to 2 hours

2 to 3 hours

3 to 4 hours

over a weekend

LEVEL OF DIFFICULTY

Easy – Little skill required; great for beginners (hard to mess up).

Moderate - Some skill required; a little more complicated.

Advanced - Requires some skill and time to complete.

Although wreaths labeled "moderate" and "advanced" take more skill, don't be afraid to tackle any of them - just study the photos and follow the instructions. As you work, make adjustments for your individual style. Above all, have fun and remember there are no mistakes - only opportunities for a creative adventure.

Wire Frame Wreaths

Wire frame wreaths are lightweight, sturdy, and inexpensive so they are a good choice for many types of wreaths. Items can be wedged between the wires or bound to the frame with wire. Wire frames work well with dried materials (like the Lavender Wreath) and fresh materials (like the Lemon Leaf Wreath). They are a favorite frame for Christmas evergreen wreaths.

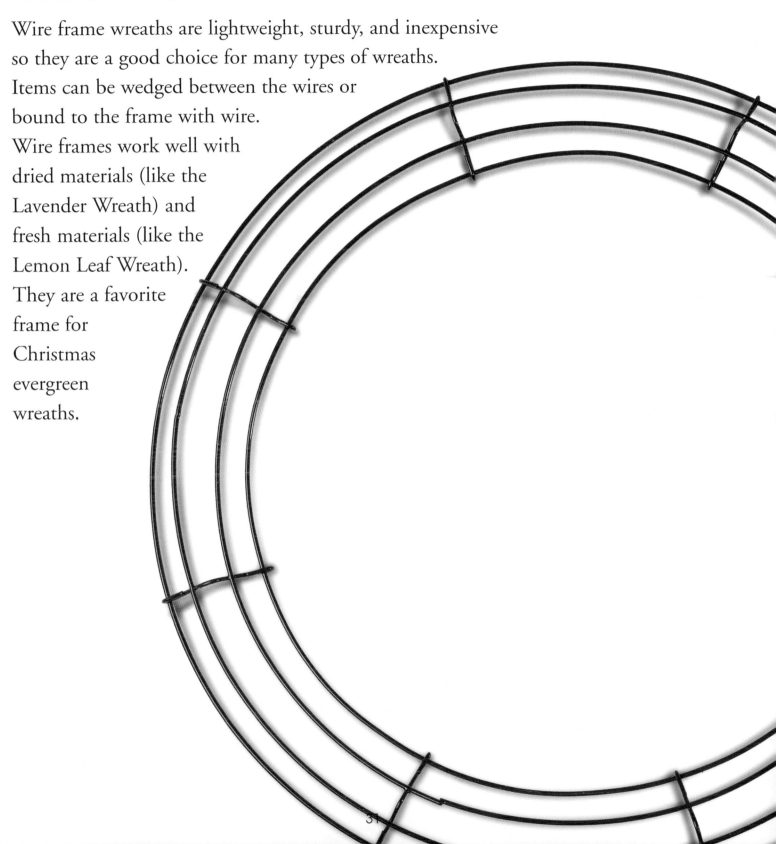

Pinecone Wreath

Pinecone wreaths are always a favorite. Whether you gather your own pinecones or purchase them, with a little time and effort you can create a beautiful wreath that will last for years.

Level of difficulty ❋ ❋

Time to complete ⏰ ⏰ ⏰ ⏰

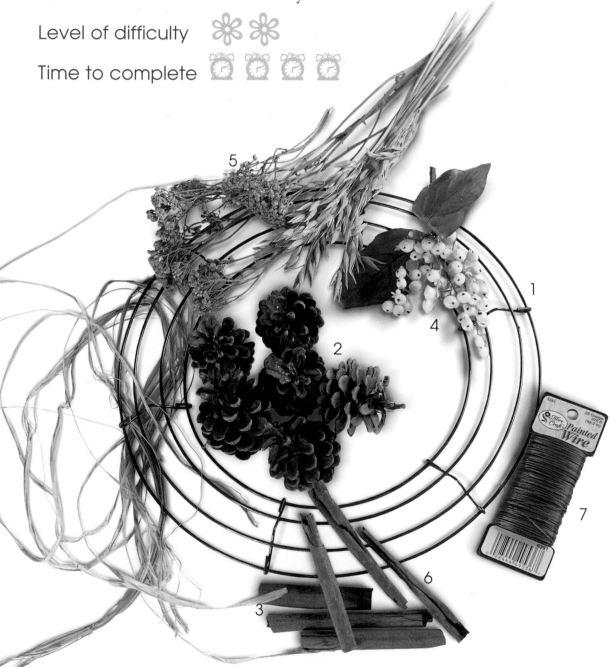

Pictured above: 1. Wire wreath frame, 2. Pinecones, 3. Cinnamon sticks, 4. Tallow berries, 5. Dried yarrow, 6. Natural raffia, 7. Wire.

SUPPLIES & TOOLS

Wire wreath frame, 12"

Pinecones, small and medium, about 65

Cinnamon sticks, 4" long, enough for four bunches

Tallow berries

Dried yarrow

Natural raffia

Wire paddle

Chenille stem

Glue gun and glue

Wire cutters

Scissors

Optional: Glossy wood-tone spray

INSTRUCTIONS

Attach Cones to Frame:

1. Working with either damp or dry pinecones, attach a floral wire around the base of each cone, wrapping the wire around the cone and twisting the wire at the base. (photo 1)

Photo 1. Attach the wire to a cone.

2. Starting on the outside edge, wrap wired cones to the wreath frame, twisting the wires tightly. (photo 2) Run the wire back and forth across the frame for more security. (photo 3) Use pliers, if needed, to make the wire secure, then twist ends and cut. (photo 4)

3. Continue working around the frame, wiring the cones very close together. Overlap some or add a second layer, if desired. If you are using damp cones, they will expand as they dry.

4. *Option:* Spray dry cones with glossy wood tone spray if they appear dull or discolored.

Add Accents:

1. Make four clusters of cinnamon sticks. Tie them in the center with natural raffia.

2. Glue and wire cinnamon stick clusters to the wreath. (photo 5)

3. Glue berries around each cinnamon stick cluster. (photo 6)

4. Cut short lengths of yarrow and glue around each cinnamon stick cluster. (photo 7)

Add Bow & Hanger:

1. Form raffia into a multiple loop bow with 3" loops and 10" streamers. Glue and wire raffia bow to the 1 o'clock position on the wreath.

2. Glue berries and yarrow in the center of the bow.

3. Form a chenille stem into a loop and attach to top back of wreath as a hanger.

Photo 2. Attach a cone to the wreath frame.

Photo 3. Run the wire across the frame for security.

Photo 4. Twist the ends of the wire to secure.

Photo 5. Wire a cinnamon stick cluster to wreath.

Photo 6. Glue in tallow berries.

Photo 7. Glue in dried yarrow.

Design Variation

Spray the cones with metallic spray paint (gold or silver or copper) after they are attached to the wire frame for a beautiful effect.

Designer's Tip

For a full-looking wreath, soak the pinecones in water, which causes them to close. Attach them to the wreath when they are closed and damp. As they dry, they will open again.

Christmas Ornament Wreath

No matter what color combination you choose, this wreath of shiny Christmas ornaments is a reflective beauty. A combination of purples, blues, and hot pink give a contemporary feel; reds, greens, and gold are more traditional.

Level of difficulty

Time to complete

SUPPLIES & TOOLS

Wire wreath frame, 12"

Assorted Christmas ornaments, colors of choice:

24 large, 2-1/4"

30 medium, 1-1/2"

36 small, 1"

Evergreen sprigs

Floral wire

Chenille stem

Wire cutters

Glue gun and glue

INSTRUCTIONS

Attach Ornaments:

1. Starting with the largest ornaments, slip a floral wire through the hanger and twist tightly to secure.

2. Starting at the outside edge of the wreath frame, attach ornament to frame with wire, twisting wire around frame. Wire remaining large ornaments to the frame, spacing them randomly.

3. Follow with the medium ornaments, then the small ones, until the wreath is covered.

Finish:

1. Cut evergreen sprigs into short lengths. Glue sprigs between the ornaments to fill in the wreath.

2. Twist chenille stem into a loop and attach to top back of the wreath as a hanger. ❏

Fresh Idea

Use fresh evergreen instead of artificial for a wonderful fragrance. Cut evergreens will stay fresh longest if you display the wreath in a cool location and mist it lightly with water every few days.

Designer's Tips:

• *Choose ornaments carefully if you want to hang the wreath outdoors. Some ornaments will peel in damp, wet weather.*

• *The wreath looks equally at home on the wall or as a table centerpiece with a candle in the middle. It is best to use unbreakable ball ornaments with attached hangers.*

Lemon Wreath

Lemons surrounded by glossy green foliage and blossoms are a great addition to a kitchen or entry door. Made of artificial lemons on a wire base, this wreath is lightweight and easy to hang. The bright yellow color of lemons always looks happy.

Level of difficulty

Time to complete

SUPPLIES & TOOLS

Wire wreath frame, 15"

Artificial lemons - 12 large, 10 medium, 10 small, 12 tiny

Bright green berries

Green snowball blossoms

Foliage (your choice) - Asparagus fern, lemon leaves, or others

Honeysuckle vine

Floral wire

Chenille stem

Wire cutters

Glue gun and glue

Awl or ice pick

INSTRUCTIONS

Attach Lemons:

1. Using an awl or ice pick, pierce a hole through the small, medium, and large lemons. (photo 1) Reserve the tiny ones.
2. Insert wire through each hole (photo 2). Put wire ends together at back of lemon and twist.
3. Beginning with the large lemons wire to wreath at random. Continue with medium and small lemons.

Attach Foliage:

1. Cut foliage into to short pieces.
2. Glue lemon leaves around the lemons as a background.
3. Fill in with asparagus fern pieces and other foliage.
4. Glue clusters of berries at random, then snowball blossoms.

Finish:

1. Glue tiny lemons at random around wreath.
2. Glue lengths of honeysuckle vine over the wreath as shown.
3. Twist a chenille stem into a loop and attach to top back of the wreath as a hanger. ❏

Lemon Facts

- *Lemons were cultivated in Palestine as early as the first century.*
- *Ladies of Louis XIV's court rubbed lemons on their lips to produce a rosy glow.*

Design Variation

Use oranges instead of lemons.

Designer's Tip

You can substitute fresh lemons for the artifical ones using the same technique for attaching a wire. Be sure you choose a sturdy wire frame as the lemons will be heavier than the artifical kind. Fill in with sprigs of fresh lemon leaves.

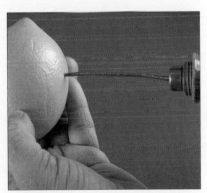

Photo 1. Piercing a lemon with an ice pick.

Photo 2. Running a wire through the holes.

Dried Wreaths

Dried flower wreaths have nostalgic charm, and they are a great way to enjoy natural flowers all year round. Many flowers can be attached to a wreath when they are fresh and allowed to dry in place - pussy willow, peony, bells of Ireland, yarrow, and bittersweet all work well. Dried flowers can be purchased at craft and florist shops, or you can try your hand at drying your own.

Though beautiful, dried flowers are sometimes considered difficult to use. Adding moisture can help reduce shattering (breakage) as you work. Try holding the flowers over a pot of boiling water before you start to assemble the wreath; the steam will make the flowers more pliable. You can also mist flowers with water as you work. With either method, test a few flowers first - some commercially dried flowers have been dyed and the color may bleed. You can save the flowers that shatter and add them to an existing potpourri.

To prolong its life, hang a dried wreath in a protected location away from bright sun where it will not be disturbed.

Pictured right: Dried Lavender Wreath. Instructions begin on page 42.

Dried Lavender Wreath

Pictured on page 41

The delightful fragrance and color of lavender makes this wreath a sensual treat. Hang it in the bedroom or bath and enjoy its calming fragrance. Choose a protected location - getting bumped by a door (or a person!) can cause the lavender to shatter.

Level of difficulty

Time to complete

SUPPLIES & TOOLS

Wire wreath frame, 12"
Dried lavender
Floral tape
Wire
Chenille stem
Cutters
Glue

INSTRUCTIONS

1. Cluster small bunches of lavender and cut to about 6" in length using pruning shears. (photo 1)

2. Bind with floral tape near the stems' ends. (photo 2)

3. Starting at the 2 o'clock position on the wreath frame, bind bunches of lavender to the wreath frame with wire. (photo 3) Add more bunches to the wreath, overlapping the heads slightly. Continue to add lavender bunches around the wreath until the frame is covered. Tuck the ends of

Photo 1. Trimming the stems of a lavender bunch.

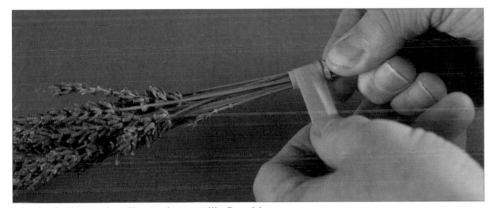

Photo 2. Wrapping them stems with floral tape.

the last clusters under the heads of the first ones as you move to the end.

4. Glue additional clusters of lavender flowers as needed to add fullness and fill gaps.

5. Attach a chenille stem to top back as a hanger. ❑

Photo 3. Attaching lavender bunches to the wreath frame with wire.

Designer's Tip

Mist the lavender with water as you work to make it more pliable and reduce shattering. Save the buds that fall for making sachets.

Fresh Tip

If you grow your own lavender or have access to fresh lavender make this wreath with fresh lavender, and allow it to dry in place. Make the wreath extra full because the lavender will shrink as it dries. While the wreath is drying, keep it out of bright sun or hot locations.

Lavender Facts

- *There are over 50 different species of lavender; the most common are the English and French varieties. Lavender flowers may be pink, white, purple, or blue.*

- *Prized for its fragrance, lavender is often used in aromatherapy to relive stress, treat headaches, and aid relaxation.*

- *Years ago, it was used as a condiment for flavoring food and to digestion. (You will find it today in some Herbes de Provence blends.)*

- *Today, lavender is used in perfumes and in pharmaceuticals to cover unpleasant odors in ointments and creams.*

Hydrangea Wreath

Hydrangeas are always impressive with their full, lush shape and tiny blossoms. Whether you make this wreath with dried or silk hydrangeas, it will be classically beautiful. If you use dried flowers, choose a dried foam wreath frame - it will be easier to insert the stems. You can also use fresh hydrangea blossoms and let them dry in place on the wreath.

Level of difficulty

Time to complete

SUPPLIES & TOOLS

Extruded foam wreath (for silk flowers) or dried foam wreath (for dried or fresh flowers), 14"

Hydrangea blossoms - 12 to 15 large heads

1-1/2 yds. moss green silk ribbon, 2-1/2" wide

Glue

Floral wire

Scissors

Wood picks (if using dried or fresh flowers)

U-pins

Optional (for dried flowers): Water mister bottle

INSTRUCTIONS

Attach Flowers:

1. If using dried or fresh hydrangeas, attach wood picks to clusters of blossoms and secure with floral tape. (Silks can be inserted directly into the wreath.) *Option:* Lightly mist dried blossoms with water to make them more pliable.
2. Starting at the 2 o'clock position on the frame and working counter-clockwise, insert blossom at a slight angle. Continue inserting flowers until the whole wreath is covered. Step back as you work to see that the wreath frame is covered evenly.

Add Ribbon:

1. Cut a 1-yard length of green silk ribbon. Pin and glue each end, equally spaced, on the back of the wreath.
2. Twist a small loop in the top center of the ribbon for a hanger. Secure with a floral wire.
3. Form the remaining ribbon into a two-loop bow. Secure at the center with wire and attach just below the hanger loop. Trim ends of ribbon into V-shapes.
4. *Option:* Glue a couple of flowers in the center of the bow. ❑

Fresh Tip

Fresh hydrangea can be glued into a grape vine wreath and allowed to dry in place. Or use a dried foam wreath into which you insert the fresh hydrangeas. Try using small bits of hydrangea, either fresh or dried, on miniature wreaths; these make beautiful package accents and ornaments.

Hydrangea Facts

• *Color - Hydrangeas can be a range of colors, from blue to purple to pink. Acid soil (you can acidify soil by adding aluminum sulfate) produces blue blooms; sweet soil (sweeten by adding lime) produces pink blooms.*

• *Drying - To dry fresh hydrangeas, remove the leaves. Bundle five or six together with rubberbands and hang in a cool, dry place.*

Hydrangeas also will dry in a vase. Place the stems in a vase with a few inches of water, out of direct sunlight. As the water evaporates add more, repeating until the blooms are dry.

Gourmet Kitchen Wreath

Fresh garlic cloves and dried red peppers, Sweet Annie, and bay leaves appear ready for a wonderful recipe - and they are! The wreath materials can be used and replaced - or simply make the wreath as a wonderful accent or as a gift for a friend who loves to cook.

Level of difficulty

Time to complete

SUPPLIES & TOOLS

Purchased greenery wreath, 18" *or* make your own by attaching a greens garland to a wire frame

14 garlic heads

36 dried red peppers

Bay leaves

Sweet Annie

Chenille stem

Glue

INSTRUCTIONS

1. Twist chenille stem into a loop on top back of the wreath as a hanger.

2. Shape greenery on the wreath to create a full lush appearance.

3. Remove the loose outer papery skins from the garlic heads so they will stay in place when glued. Using the photo as a guide, glue four clusters of garlic heads to the wreath.

4. Glue red peppers and bay leaves around each garlic cluster.

5. Fill in around each garlic cluster with pieces of sweet Annie. ❑

Designer's Tip

If you use any of the materials as food, be sure to cut off any glue.

Garlic Facts

• *Garlic is a culinary herb that's been called the wonder drug of all the herbs. The same chemicals that give garlic its strong odor destroy and inhibit the growth of certain bacteria and fungi.*

• *Garlic has a longstanding reputation as a vampire retardant.*

Eucalyptus Wreath

Its rich color and earthy fragrance make preserved eucalyptus a favorite for wreaths. This wreath is easy to create - it uses an extruded foam wreath and floral U-pins. Roses, trailing greenery, and braided cord with tassels give the wreath a dressy look.

Level of difficulty

Time to complete

SUPPLIES & TOOLS

16 oz. brown eucalyptus

Extruded foam wreath frame, 12"

2 yellow open roses with buds

Trailing greenery (your choice)

2 yds. braided cord with tassels

Birch twigs

Chenille stem

Glue

U-pins

INSTRUCTIONS

Attach Eucalyptus & Twigs:

1. Twist a chenille stem into a loop and insert and glue at the top back of the wreath as a hanger.

2. Cut eucalyptus into 6" lengths. Starting at the 2 o'clock position, lay a cluster of five or six stems on the wreath and pin in place with floral U-pin. Secure pin with glue.

3. Continue pinning clusters of eucalyptus around the wreath, working counter clockwise, allowing the clusters to overlap slightly.

4. Insert and glue birch twigs randomly around the wreath, using the photo as a guide for placement.

Add Accents:

1. Insert and glue a cluster of trailing greens at the bottom center of the wreath.

2. Insert and glue roses and buds as shown.

3. Pin and glue the braid with tassels to the wreath, starting at the top edge, looping the braid around the wreath and allowing it to extend below the bottom of the wreath. ❑

Eucalyptus Facts:

• *A native of Australia, eucalyptus is an evergreen tree that is cultivated worldwide. It is popular in floral design and widely used medicinally.*

• *Aborigines chewed the roots as a source of water and made the leaves into a tea that was used to help cure high fevers.*

Grains & Grasses Wreath

Subtle shades of amber, gold, and green give this wreath its earthy beauty.

Level of difficulty

Time to complete

Pictured above: (1) Setaria, (2) Wheat, (3) Avena, (4) Rye, (5) China Millet, (6) Extruded foam wreath, (7) Wood picks, (8) U-pins, (9) Spray Sealer, (10) Floral tape.

Fresh Tip

Fresh cut grasses and grains can be wired to a wire wreath frame and allowed to dry in place. Because they are pliable when fresh, you will have less shattering and can more easily shape their stems. Make your wreath fuller than you want the dried wreath to be because the grains and grasses will shrink a bit as they dry.

Designer's Tip

You can tint any grass or grain with floral spray paint. Glossy wood-tone brown and basil green both work well to enhance the colors of dried grains and grasses.

continued from page 51

SUPPLIES & TOOLS

Extruded foam wreath, 12"

Assorted grains and grasses, natural and green colors - Avena, China millet, rye, wheat, setaria

Floral U-pins

Glue

Wooden floral picks

Floral tape

Pruning shears

Optional: Clear matte spray sealer

INSTRUCTIONS

1. Cut grains and grasses into 4" lengths. (photo 1)

2. Form a cluster of eight to ten stems of grains and grasses, securing the ends with floral tape. Strengthen weak stems of grasses and grains by attaching them to wood picks with floral tape. (photo 2)

3. Starting at the 2 o'clock position on the wreath frame, lay a cluster of grains and grasses on the wreath and pin in place with floral U pin. Secure pin with glue.

4. Continue pinning clusters around the wreath, moving counter-clock-wise, allowing the clusters to overlap slightly. (photo 3)

5. Glue in heads of grains as needed to create a full, lush look.

6. Twist chenille stem into a loop and attach to top back as a hanger.

7. *Option:* Spray the entire wreath with clear matte spray to help preserve the wreath and prevent shattering. ❏

Photo 1. Trimming the stems of a cluster of grains and grasses.

Photo 2. Attaching a wood pick with floral tape.

Photo 3. Securing the clusters to the wreath with U-pins.

Straw Wreaths

Straw makes a wonderfully sturdy, inexpensive wreath base. Whether you cover the straw completely or leave some of it exposed, straw is a great base for chunky, lush wreaths. Materials can be inserted, pinned, wired, or glued to straw wreath bases - just try any straw wreath project in this book and you will see how versatile straw wreath bases are.

Forest Splendor Wreath

Dried pods, cones, and reindeer moss are focal elements of the forest splendor wreath. This is an international wreath - protea is from South Africa, lotus is from Asia, and artichokes are from California. A sturdy straw base forms a strong support; small spheres of copper wire add metallic sparkle and contrast.

Level of difficulty

Time to complete

Designer's Tip

This wreath, with its rugged good looks, would look equally great in a den or at the front door.

Lotus Pod Facts

The lotus grows in water and has exquisite flowers that last only three days - as the flower fades and the petals fall away, the large seedpod is revealed at the center of each blossom.

Pictured left:
(1) Straw wreath base
(2) Sponge mushrooms
(3) Small lotus pods
(4) Pomegranates
(5) Bell cups
(6) Artichokes
(7) Pinecones
(8) Berries
(9) Grasses
(10) Copper wire
(11) Moss
(12) Pod

continued from page 55

SUPPLIES & TOOLS

Straw wreath, 14"

5 sponge mushrooms

8 small lotus pods

4 pomegranates

2 bell cups

3 artichokes

3 protea flats

8 pinecones

Assorted small berries (your choice)

Assorted dried grasses and twigs (your choice)

Green reindeer moss

Copper wire, 28 gauge

Chenille stem

Floral U-pins

Wood picks

Glue

Wire cutters

INSTRUCTIONS

Insert Dried Materials:

1. Form a chenille stem into a hanging loop and insert and glue at top back of wreath. Secure the loop with floral U-pins.

2. Cut the pod stems to 2". If some pods and cones do not have stems, glue and wire them to wood picks.

3. Insert and glue sponge mushroom, spacing equally around the outer edge of the wreath. (Sponge mushrooms that are too large can be broken into smaller pieces.)

4. Glue and insert lotus pods at a slight angle around the top and inside opening of the wreath.

5. Insert and glue bell cups in the wreath.

6. Continue with artichoke, pomegranate (photo 1), and protea flats.

7. Add cones and other pods as desired.

8. Fill in around the pods with green reindeer moss, small berries, dried grasses, and small twigs. Continue adding materials until you have full, lush-looking wreath.

Add Accents:

1. Cut eight 2-yard lengths of copper wire. Crumple each piece in your palm and roll as you would a dough ball to make a copper wire sphere. (photo 2)

2. Glue copper spheres to wreath tucked in among the pods and moss. ❑

Photo 1. Inserting a pomegranate.

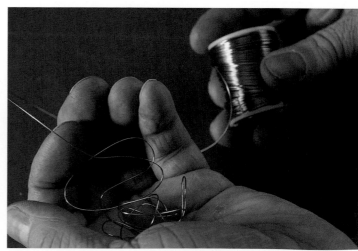

Photo 2. Making a copper wire sphere.

Seaside Wreath Centerpiece

Some wreaths - like this one - look great off the wall in the center of the table. Pretty shells, flowers, and greens surround votive candles. It's a great way to display those shells you collected at the beach.

SUPPLIES & TOOLS

Straw wreath, 14"

1 pegged votive cup, 4" tall

4 candles

Assorted seashells

3 dried-look coral roses

15 blue bachelor buttons

Blue seafoam statice

Twigs

String of pearls foliage

Pea gravel

Plastic foam scraps

Knife

Glue

Wood picks

Level of difficulty

Time to complete

INSTRUCTIONS

1. Place straw wreath on a flat surface. Using a knife, make holes for votive at 9 o'clock.
2. Glue votives into holes.
3. Starting with the largest shells and using the photo as a guide, glue shells to the wreath. Use generous amount of glue to secure shells. TIP: Glue small pieces of Styrofoam® on the backs of scallop shells, insert a wood pick in the foam, and glue to the wreath.
4. Insert and glue one coral rose to left of the 9 o'clock votive and two roses at the 3 o'clock position on wreath.
5. Glue clusters of twigs extending from the shells.
6. Fill in around the shells with bachelor buttons, seafoam statice, and string of pearls.
7. Add leaves and moss as needed to hide any glue.
8. Place a handful of pea gravel in votive cup. Place candle on top of gravel. ❑

Burst of Spring Wreath

A lush green moss wreath surrounds a beautiful collection of spring-time blossoms that look as if they have just burst forth into the warm sunshine. After a long, cold winter, the fresh colors and shapes of this wreath would be a welcome addition to any room or door.

Level of difficulty

Time to complete

Fresh Idea

After covering the straw wreath in sheet moss, attach a small piece of fresh floral foam wrapped in plastic using chenille stems for attaching. Insert flowers of your choice into the foam. When the fresh flowers fade you can remove the foam and flowers and use the moss covered wreath again.

SUPPLIES & TOOLS

Straw wreath, 14"

Green sheet moss

3 Narcissus with attached bulbs

Purple African violet cluster

White field daisies

Assorted bright green and blue small blossoms

Trailing ivy

Tallow berry stem

Artificial or dried grapevine

Reindeer moss

Chenille stem

Floral U-pins

Paddle wire

Wood picks

Optional: Green floral spray *or* green acrylic paint and spray bottle; clear matte spray sealer

INSTRUCTIONS

Cover & Prepare:

1. Soak the sheet moss in water for a few minutes to make it more pliable and restore some of its green color. Squeeze out excess water.

2. Place sections of moss across the wreath and pin in place with U-pins, continuing until the wreath is covered.

3. Attach end of paddle wire to a wood pick and insert in back of wreath. Wrap wire over top of moss every few inches to help hold it in place.

4. *Option:* If moss is not as green as you like, spray with green floral paint or green acrylic paint diluted with water and placed in a spray bottle. Let dry.

5. Twist chenille stem into a hanging loop and insert and glue to top back of wreath.

Add Florals:

1. Atach pieces of grapevine vertically in the areas on the left and right sides of wreath where flowers will be placed. Use U-pins to hold grapevine in place.

2. Insert and glue narcissus at bottom left to create a strong vertical line. Secure with U-pins as needed. These are placed on top of grapevine pieces.

3. Insert African violet in bottom center of wreath.

4. Insert and glue vertical cluster of bright green blossoms to right bottom of wreath. These are placed on top of the grapevine pieces.

5. Insert cluster of blue blossoms around the green.

6. Insert trailing ivy beneath the green flower cluster and to the left of the narcissus cluster. Shape ivy into gentle curves for a natural look.

7. Fill in with field daisies and tallow berries.

8. Glue clumps of green reindeer moss to hide pins and glue, as needed.

9. *Option:* Spray the entire wreath with clear matte spray to keep the moss from shedding. ❑

Pumpkin Patch Wreath

A straw wreath is a natural base for this harvest arrangement that features the warm colors and textures of a bright autumn day. The wood tone spray helps unify all the elements of the wreath. The natural materials and miniature pumpkins are a delightful way to greet friends and family at the front door.

Level of difficulty

Time to complete

SUPPLIES & TOOLS

Straw wreath, 12" unwrapped

Miniature artificial pumpkins

2 sponge mushroom

Orange berry sprays

Assorted autumn-colored foliage

Twigs

Moss

Glossy wood-tone spray paint

Chenille stem

Wood picks

Glue

INSTRUCTIONS

1. Make a loop from a chenille stem. Insert loop in the top back of the wreath as a hanger.

2. Insert pick in bottom of each pumpkin. Insert and glue two larger pumpkins, centered at the bottom of the wreath.

3. Insert and glue sponge mushrooms terraced below the pumpkins. (The mushrooms should extend in front of the wreath.)

4. Insert and glue clusters of orange berries to the right and left of the pumpkins.

5. Insert and glue foliage and berries around the pumpkins, allowing some of the materials to cascade forward.

6. Insert and glue remaining pumpkins.

7. Glue mosses to fill empty spots and hide any glue.

8. Lightly spray entire wreath with glossy wood-tone spray. ❑

Pumpkin Facts

- *Pumpkins can range in size from one pound to many. The largest ever grown was 1,140 pounds.*

- *Native Americans used pumpkin seeds as both food and medicine.*

- *Pumpkins have even been flattened, dried, and made into mats.*

Extruded Foam Wreaths

Extruded foam wreaths are often mistakenly referred to as plastic foam (Styrofoam®) wreaths, but do not be fooled - they have their own unique qualities. Extruded foam wreaths are made of smooth, dense foam so they're perfect for painting and gluing. In green or white, they are a great choice for many wreaths because they are lightweight, making insertions easy.

Coffee Bean Delight Wreath

The beautiful aroma, color, shape, and texture of coffee beans turn a plain extruded wreath into a warm and friendly greeting. It's easy to create with a few simple materials. Any coffee lover would enjoy this wreath on a wall or as a centerpiece with a candle in the center.

Level of difficulty

Time to complete

SUPPLIES & TOOLS

Extruded foam wreath, 10"

Acrylic craft paint - Brown

Coffee beans

3 yds. copper-color beaded cord trim

Grapes and berries, assorted colors

Brown leaves

Foam brush, 1"

Chenille stem

Strong all-purpose adhesive *or* white craft glue (Do NOT use hot glue.)

Glue spreader (craft stick)

Floral U-pins

INSTRUCTIONS

Cover Foam:

1. Using the foam brush, paint foam wreath base with brown acrylic paint. Apply two coats, allowing drying time between and after the second coat.
2. Make a loop from a chenille stem. Attach loop to top back as a hanger.
3. Working one small section at a time, apply a heavy layer of glue to the wreath. (photo 1) Press coffee beans into the glue. (photo 2) Continue applying glue and coffee beans until entire wreath is covered. Allow to dry overnight.

Add Accents:

1. Glue and pin with U-pins a cluster of brown leaves to the top of the wreath.
2. Form the beaded trim into a four-loop bow with 3" loops and 14" streamers.
3. Pin and glue bow at center of leaf cluster.
4. Insert and glue grapes in the center of the bow.
5. Pin and glue bow streamers to bottom of wreath.
6. Glue berries around the streamers. ❏

Photo 1

Photo 2

Designer's Tip

A wreath this size is great as a centerpiece. To use as a centerpiece, place wreath flat on the table and insert a small saucer in the center. Place a candle on the saucer and sprinkle some loose coffee beans around the base of the candle.

Coffee Facts

- *More than half (52%) of the adult population of the United States drinks coffee every day. That's 107 million daily drinkers.*

- *The coffee plant is a large bush with dark green, oval-shaped leaves. It can reach a height of 14 to 20 feet when fully grown.*

Exotic Orchid Wreath

The look of an exotic island is easy to create with a few flowers, river cane, and an extruded foam wreath base. If you dream of an exotic destination or want a tropical touch for your decor, this wreath fits the bill.

Level of difficulty

Time to complete

SUPPLIES & TOOLS

Extruded foam wreath, 12"

Acrylic craft paints - Avocado green, leaf green, olive green, moon yellow, terra cotta

Small natural sea sponge

Foam brush, 1"

Disposable foam plate

River cane or bamboo

Phalaenopsis orchid

Orchid foliage

Spider plant foliage

Bear grass

Reindeer moss

Chenille stem

Straight pins

INSTRUCTIONS

Paint & Prepare:
1. Squeeze a small puddle of leaf green paint on a foam plate. Using the foam brush, paint entire wreath with two coats of leaf green, allowing the paint to dry between and after the final coat.
2. Squeeze small puddles of other paint colors on the plate. Wet the sponge and squeeze out excess water. Dip moist sponge randomly in the paint colors. Pounce the sponge on the plate to blend colors slightly and sponge colors on the wreath, creating a mottled look. Allow to dry.
3. Twist a chenille stem into a loop. Insert and glue loop in the top back of the wreath as a hanger.

Add River Cane:
1. Cut six sections of river cane into lengths between 12" and 18". Cut two river cane sections 10" long and three sections between 4" and 5".
2. Glue and pin three of the longest river canes to back left side of wreath and three to the front right side.
3. Glue and pin two 10" lengths horizontally at middle bottom of wreath. Glue and pin small section across top right front of wreath.

Add Florals:
1. Insert and glue an orchid section on left side of wreath. Insert another orchid section, cascading downward, on left side. Insert and glue a small section of orchid near the top right of the wreath.
2. Fill in around the flowers with orchid foliage, spider plant leaves, and bear grass.
3. Glue clumps of green reindeer moss to add texture and cover any visible glue. ❏

Fresh Idea

Make a "growing wreath". After painting the extruded foam wreath and attaching the river cane, consider adding small air growing plants or miniature tropical plants in pots to the wreath. Cover the pots with Spanish moss.

Orchid Facts

• *There are about 30,000 species of orchids, making them one of the largest groups of flowering plants.*

• *Orchids are found in every climate except deserts. In their natural growing conditions orchids are dependent on a specific insect to be pollinated.*

Blooming Reflection Wreath

Tulips and an inspirational "bloom" sign decorate this fun wreath. It would be great in a powder room or on a wall that needs a bit of reflective color.

Level of difficulty

Time to complete

SUPPLIES & TOOLS

Extruded foam wreath, 12"

Round mirror, 12" diameter

3 large pink tulips

Wooden letters, 4" tall, to spell "BLOOM"

Galax leaves

Bear grass

Trailing foliage

Reindeer moss

Cardboard, 10" x 3"

Pink and purple floral-print paper, 8-1/2" x 11"

Acrylic craft paint - Purple

Small artist's paint brush

Plastic foam (Styrofoam®), 2" x 2"

Glue

Floral U-pins

Floral wire

INSTRUCTIONS

Make the Sign:
1. Using the artist's brush, paint the letters with purple acrylic paint. Use two coats and allow drying between coats and after the second coat.
2. Wrap the cardboard with floral print paper and secure paper with glue.
3. Glue letters, spacing them equally, on the paper-covered cardboard.

Cover the Wreath:
1. Put glue around the outer edge of the mirror. Position wreath on mirror. Allow glue to dry.
2. Remove any plastic veins from the galax leaves. Working one leaf at a time, put a thin layer of heavy white craft glue on back of leaf and apply to wreath. Allow some of the leaves to slightly overlap the mirror. Continue until the entire wreath is covered.

Decorate:
1. Form the tulips and bear grass into a staggered cluster, using the photo as a guide. Twist a floral wire around the cluster to secure.
2. Using floral U-pins and glue attach tulips and bear grass cluster to left side of wreath.
3. Glue and pin Styrofoam® on top of binding point (the place where they are secured with wire) on the tulips.
4. Glue sign on top of the Styrofoam®, adjusting as needed before the glue dries so the word is level.
5. Pin and glue trailing foliage around the wreath.
6. Glue clumps of green reindeer moss to hide glue and foam. ❏

Tulip Facts

• *Tulips, which are the world's most widely grown bulb, have more than 3,500 varieties and species. Most of the tulips in the world come from The Netherlands.*

• *Fresh cut tulip flowers, placed in water, will continue to grow toward the light.*

• *Tulips come in almost every color except black.*

• *In Victorian times, the gift of a red tulip was a declaration of love.*

Plastic Foam Wreaths

You can add texture, carve, paint, glue, or cover plastic foam (Styrofoam®) wreath bases to create almost any effect. (And plain white ones are a great background for snowy wreaths.) Because plastic foam wreath bases will break with a lot of weight or heavy insertions, I glue cardboard or mat board to the back of the wreath for support.

Pictured right: Summer Vegetable Garden Wreath. Instructions begin on page 72

Summer Vegetable Garden Wreath

Pictured on page 71

The brightly colored artificial vegetables contrast with the dark earth tones, making this wreath a nice choice for a kitchen or covered patio.

Level of difficulty

Time to complete

SUPPLIES & TOOLS

Plastic foam (Styrofoam®) wreath, 14" x 2"

Floral spray paints - Black, dark brown, glossy wood-tone

Artificial vegetables:

   2 scallions

   Tomato

   Green pepper

   2 carrots

   2 radishes

   2 mushrooms - 1 large, 1 small

   4 stalks asparagus

Assorted variegated foliage

Yellow filler flowers

Artificial or dried grapevine

Bear grass

Reindeer moss

1 yd. natural woven ribbon, 1-1/2" wide

Chenille stem

Knife

Floral U-pins

Wood picks

INSTRUCTIONS

Prepare & Paint Wreath:

1. Using a knife cut small chunks from the edges of the wreath base, cutting grooves in the top and sides of the wreath to create an uneven texture. (photo 1) Brush away any loose particles.

2. Working in a well-ventilated area and following the package instructions, spray the wreath with short bursts of black and brown paint. Allow the colors to overlap.

3. Spray entire wreath with glossy wood-tone spray. Allow to dry.

4. Make a hanger from a chenille stem and insert hanger in the top back of the wreath.

Add Vegetables, Foliage & Bow:

1. Using floral U-pins, pin and glue scallions to the middle left side of wreath.

2. Insert pick in bottom of tomato. (photo 2) Insert and glue tomato in bottom center of wreath. (photo 3)

3. Insert pick in bottom of green pepper. Insert and glue to right and above tomato.

4. Form the ribbon into a two-loop bow with 3" loops. Insert and glue bow on a diagonal to the left of the tomato.

5. Insert a pick in the back of each carrot and radish. Insert and glue them beneath the tomato and green pepper, allowing one carrot to rest on top of the bow.

6. Fill in around the vegetables with foliage. (photo 4) Insert asparagus and mushrooms.

7. Form bear grass into a loop and secure in place with a wood pick. Insert vertically on right side of wreath.

8. Twist and curl artificial grapevine around the wreath, holding it in place with glue and floral U-pins.

9. Glue clumps of reindeer moss to cover U-pins and glue.

10. Insert filler flowers in some moss clumps. ❏

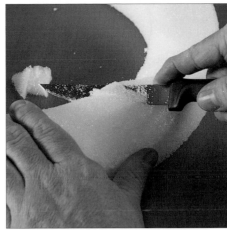

Photo 1. Carving the wreath base.

Photo 2. Inserting a pick in a tomato.

Photo 3. Inserting the tomato in the wreath.

Photo 4. Inserting foliage around the vegetables.

Designer Tips

• *If you cannot find artificial grapevine, wrap floral wire with brown floral tape, making the tape thicker in some sections and thinner in others. Spray lightly with glossy wood-tone spray.*

• *If the colors of the vegetables seem too bright, lightly spray them with glossy wood-tone spray to mute the colors and give an antiqued look.*

• *Variation: Use all one vegetable (like peas) and add seed packets and small clay pots.*

Mille fleur Wreath

The variety of flowers, colors, and textures of this wreath make it a beautiful focal point for spring and summer. It's a great wreath to make when you have flower heads that have fallen from their stems, flowers with short stems, and odds and ends of blossoms - or purchase bushes and mixed sprays of flowers to yield a large quantity of flowers economically.

Level of difficulty

Time to complete

SUPPLIES & TOOLS

Plastic foam (Styrofoam®) wreath, 14" x 2"

Green floral paint

Silk flowers (your choice) - Mass, form, and filler flowers such as roses, hydrangea, daisy

Ivy sprigs

Chenille stem

Wood picks

Glue

Knife

INSTRUCTIONS

Paint Wreath:
1. Slightly bevel the edges of the foam wreath with a knife. Smooth edges with a scrap of Styrofoam.
2. Make a hanger with a chenille stem and attach hanger to top back of wreath base.
3. Working in a well-ventilated area and following the package instructions, spray the wreath base with moss green paint. Allow to dry. Repeat.

Add Flowers:
1. Attach flowers to wood picks if the stems are short or are difficult to insert in the wreath base.
2. Starting with the largest flowers, insert and glue blossoms around the wreath, spacing them equally.
3. Insert the next largest flowers around the largest flowers, inserting a few around the inside and outside edges of the wreath. Create a balance of color and sizes.
4. Continue adding flowers, ending with smallest ones, until wreath is totally covered. TIP: Glue the smallest blossoms to the edges of some of the larger flowers.
5. Insert sprigs of ivy as desired. ❑

Fresh Idea

Using a grapevine wreath, insert fresh blossoms among the vines and allow to dry in place. Roses, hydrangea, and other garden flowers will all dry nicely. When the flowers are dry you can add in commercially dried filler flowers as needed for a lush look that will last and last.

Designer's Tip

To create a unified look, choose flowers that are closely related in color and value. Using a variety of form, mass, and filler flowers will create textural interest. Keep the flowers close to the wreath surface and densely packed for a full, lush look.

Design Variation

Use all one type of flower (like geraniums or roses) in various sizes or colors.

Beach Cottage Wreath

Crisp white rope, seashells, and bright red blooms create a wreath that says seaside cottage. I can see it on a cottage door, on a boat, or anywhere you want a bit of seaside charm.

Level of difficulty

Time to complete

Design Variation

Use fishing bobbers and lures instead of starfish and shells. Mount a favorite vacation photo in the wreath opening.

SUPPLIES & TOOLS

Plastic foam wreath, 14" x 2"

30 ft. white *or* natural hemp rope, 3/8"

Starfish, 6"

Seashell

Geranium blossoms (red mass flower)

Dark blue seafoam statice (blue mass flower)

Foxtail grass (line flower)

Tiny yellow daisies (filler flower)

2 yds. blue denim ribbon with red edges, 1-1/2" wide

Chenille stem

Straight pins

Glue gun and glue *or* heavy white craft glue

INSTRUCTIONS

Cover Wreath Base:

1. Insert chenille stem in top back as a hanger.

2. Starting on the outside edge of the wreath base, coil the rope around the wreath and glue in place with low temperature hot glue or heavy white craft glue. Secure with straight pins. Continue coiling the rope until the outer and inner edges and face are covered, ending on the inside edge.

Decorate:

1. Insert and glue a pick in back of the starfish. Insert and glue starfish to upper left top of wreath, slightly off center.

2. Form ribbon into a two-loop bow with 4" loops and 18" streamers. Glue bow in place, nestling it to the right of the starfish.

3. Insert and glue foxtail grass, letting the grass cascade down the left side of the wreath. Repeat on the top right of the wreath.

4. Insert and glue geranium blossoms around the starfish and the bow.

5. Insert and glue seafoam statice as shown.

6. Fill in with clusters of small daisies.

7. Glue shell at inside bottom of wreath, slightly right of center.

8. Glue blossoms around the seashell.

9. Shape ribbon streamers into gentle cascades and glue in place. Trim ends of ribbon into V-shapes. ❏

Vine Wreaths

If you want a natural looking background for your wreath, grapevine is the base of choice. Pre-made grapevine wreaths are a fast, easy way to craft a wreath. They can be decorated by inserting flowers and greenery between the vines as well as by gluing and wiring. Grapevine wreaths are great for use indoors and out and are a good choice for large-scale wreaths. Best of all, you can use grapevine wreath bases over and over again by simply removing the decorations and replacing them with new ones.

Vine wreaths are easy to make yourself from a wide range of vine material such as grapevine, honeysuckle, kudzu, wisteria, etc. Wrap fresh cut vines into a circle. Tie together with hemp cord in several places and allow to dry in a dry place.

Pictured right: Summer Potting Shed Wreath. Instructions begin on page 80.

Summer Potting Shed Wreath

A loose, airy grapevine wreath is the perfect base for this collection of terra cotta pots and bright flowers. The casual placement creates a pleasant country-style wreath. It would look great in a country kitchen or at the front door.

Level of difficulty

Time to complete

SUPPLIES & TOOLS

Grapevine wreath, 14"

4 terra cotta pots, 3"

5 terra cotta pots, 2"

Grape hyacinth (line flower)

Red geranium (mass flower)

Yellow filler flowers

Assorted variegated foliage and ivy

Flower bulb with foliage

Bear grass

Reindeer moss

Spanish moss

Chenille stem

Glue gun and glue

Pruning shears

Optional: Wooden picks

INSTRUCTIONS

Prepare Wreath & Glue Pots:

1. Cut vines that bind the grapevine wreath together. (photo 1) Open up the wreath a bit so it has a loose, airy appearance, cutting away vines as needed.

2. Apply a generous amount of hot glue to the base of one 3" terra cotta pot and insert the pot diagonally among the vines at the bottom of the wreath. Using the photo as a guide, glue and insert the remaining 3" pots (photo 2), followed by the 2" pots. Do not be too concerned with glue that shows; it will be covered with moss later. *Option:* Insert a wooden pick in the hole at the bottom of the pot for more security.

Add Florals:

All florals are glued to the wreath; stems are wedged between the vines.

1. Insert and glue a vertical cluster of grape hyacinth at the bottom center of the wreath. Add a cluster of grape hyacinth cascading down the right side of the wreath.

2. Glue the flower bulb in the pot at the bottom of the wreath.

3. Shorten the stems of the geranium blossoms and glue them nestled around the pots.

4. Fill in the wreath with variegated foliage, bear grass, and ivy.

5. Glue sprigs of yellow filler flowers.

6. Glue clumps of green reindeer and Spanish moss around and inside some of the pots, and use the mosses to hide glue and add textural interest.

7. Twist a chenille stem around a few vines on the top back of the wreath as a hanger. ❏

Design Variation

Change this to an autumn-themed wreath by using mums, nuts, and colored leaves.

Photo 1. Using pruning shears to cut the vines that bind the wreath.

Photo 2. Gluing the pots in place.

Green Apple & Pear Wreath

Artificial green apples, pears, and green flowers are studded on a grapevine wreath, creating a fresh, cool look. The monochromatic color scheme would be a refreshing accent for almost any room.

Level of difficulty

Time to complete

SUPPLIES & TOOLS

Grapevine wreath, 18"

6 green apples

3 green pears

12 green crabapples

Green viburnum

Assorted gray-green foliage

Reindeer moss

Chenille stem

Drill and drill bit *or* ice pick

Wooden picks

Glue gun and glue

Pruning shears

INSTRUCTIONS

Prepare:
1. Cut a few vines from the wreath and set aside.
2. Twist a chenille stem on the top back of the wreath as a hanger.
3. Drill or punch a small hole in what will be the back of each apple and pear. (photo 1)
4. In each hole, insert a wood pick. Secure with glue. (photo 2)

Add Fruits & Florals:
1. Insert and glue the apples to the wreath, spacing them randomly and positioning the apples so they point in different directions.
2. Insert and glue pears between the apples.
3. Cut viburnum into short lengths. Insert and glue them, equally distributed, around the wreath.
4. Fill in among the apples and pears with crabapples.
5. Glue short sprigs of foliage to the wreath, using the photo as a guide.
6. Glue clumps of green reindeer moss to add texture and hide any glue.
7. Insert and glue the reserved cut vines around outside edge of wreath to create a light, airy feel. ❏

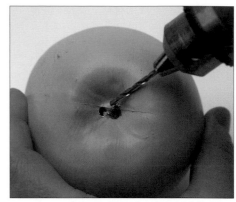

Photo 1. Using a drill to make a hole in an apple.

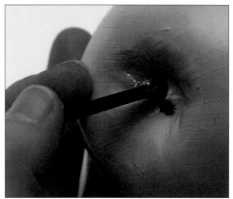

Photo 2. Inserting a wood pick in the hole.

Design Variations

- *For a warm, cozy-looking wreath, try red apples, red pears, and cream-colored blossoms.*

- *Make it a Christmas wreath by using red apples, pinecones, and evergreen sprigs.*

Spring Easy Change
Wreath

Easy Change Seasonal Wreath

It is fun to have a wreath for each season, but you may not want to go to the trouble or expense of creating and storing several wreaths. Here is a solution. A basic grapevine wreath is embellished with easy-to-remove seasonal accents, so you have one wreath many looks. What a great housewarming or wedding gift!

Level of difficulty

Time to complete

SUPPLIES & TOOLS

Grapevine wreath, 18"

Trailing green vines - your choice

Plastic foam (Styrofoam®) blocks, 2" x 2" (one for each seasonal accent)

Wooden picks

Chenille stem

Glue gun and glue

For the Spring wreath:

Flocked bunny, 6" tall

3 yds. pastel patterned ribbon, 1-1/2" wide

2-1/2 yds. pink sheer ribbon, 1-1/2" wide

Pink foxglove *or* other line flower

Pink hydrangea *or* other mass flower

Assorted pink and purple blossoms *or* other filler flowers

For the Summer wreath:

7 black-eyed Susans *or* other form flowers

Assorted grasses and green foliage *or* other line flowers

3 yds. bright green ribbon, 1-1/2" wide

For the Autumn wreath:

Scarecrow, 11" tall

2 tiny pumpkins

Orange berry sprigs

Twigs

Assorted orange-colored blossoms

2 yds. plaid ribbon in autumn colors, 1-1/2" wide

INSTRUCTIONS

Add Foliage:

1. At about the 8 o'clock position, insert and glue a cluster of green trailing foliage. Allow some foliage to trail downward.
2. At about the 1 o'clock position, insert and glue a tight cluster of trailing greens.
3. Twist a chenille stem into a loop on top back of the wreath as a hanger.

Add Spring Accents:

1. Insert and glue a wood pick in a plastic foam block. On the opposite side of the block, glue the bunny to the plastic foam.
2. Cut a 1-yard length of pastel patterned ribbon and an 18" length of pink sheer ribbon. Form each into a two-loop bow. Glue the pink bow on top of the patterned bow. Attach a wood pick to the back. Glue a pink blossom in the center of the bow. Trim ends of ribbon into V-shape. Set aside.
3. Form the remaining patterned ribbon into a two-loop bow with 4" loops. Form pink sheer ribbon into a two-loop bow with 3" loops. Center the pink bow on the patterned bow and glue together. Insert and glue the bow below the bunny. Glue hydrangea blossom in center of bow.
4. Trim pink foxglove to a height of about 10". Insert and glue foxglove vertically.
5. Fill in around bunny with assorted pink and purple blossoms.
6. Insert bunny cluster into wreath over lower greenery.
7. Insert reserved bow into wreath over upper greenery.

To remove accents: Simply lift out. ❑

Continued on next page

Fresh Idea

Attach a small bud vase or other container that will hold water to a grapevine wreath by either wedging it among the vines or gluing in place. Fill the vase with water and add in a few fresh flowers. Small glass jars look charming on a country style wreath.

continued from pag 85

Summer Easy Change Wreath

See supply list on page 85.

Add Summer Accents:

1. Insert and glue a wood pick in the back of a plastic foam (Styrofoam®) block. This pick will be used to insert into vine wreath. On the front of block, insert and glue an arrangement of six black-eyed Susans.

2. Cut a 1-yard length of green ribbon. Form into a two-loop bow. Attach to a wood pick. Glue a black-eyed Susan in the center of the bow. Set aside.

3. Form remaining green ribbon into a four-loop bow. Glue bow to flower cluster as shown. Trim ends of ribbons in V-shapes.

4. Insert foliage and grass among the black-eyed Susans.

5. Insert flower cluster in wreath over lower greenery.

6. Insert reserved bow into wreath over upper greenery.

To remove accents: Simply lift out. ❏

Autumn Easy Change Wreath

See supply list on page 85.

Add Autumn Accents:

1. Insert and glue a wood pick in a plastic foam (Styrofoam®) block. On the side opposite the pick, insert and glue scarecrow.

2. Form plaid ribbon into a four-loop bow. Trim ends of ribbon into V-shapes. Glue bow at base of scarecrow.

3. Glue pumpkins in the center of the bow.

4. Insert and glue twigs, berries, and orange flower blossoms around the scarecrow.

5. Insert scarecrow cluster into wreath over lower greenery.

To remove accents: Simply lift out. ❑

Winter Holiday Variation

Use evergreen foliage or holly instead of greens. Add a Santa, angel, or snowman with a coordinating ribbon.

Summer Centerpiece Wreath

No wall to display a wreath? Here is a clever solution - a freestanding wreath decorated with summer lilies, stock, and cascading greens. It's an easy-to-make attention getter.

Level of difficulty

Time to complete

SUPPLIES & TOOLS

Grapevine wreath, 14"

Clay saucer, 8"

Plastic foam (Styrofoam®) block, 6" x 2"

3 sponge mushrooms

2 pink lilies (form flower)

2 purple stock (line flower)

Mauve hydrangea (mass flower)

Green snowball (mass flower)

Purple filler flowers

Assorted cascading foliage

Wood picks

Floral U-pins

Knife

Glue

INSTRUCTIONS

Prepare:

1. Using a knife, trim foam block to fit inside saucer. Glue in place.

2. Place wreath, vertically centered, on plastic foam. Wedge wood picks through the wreath into the foam block. Use several picks and generous amounts of glue so the wreath is secure in the block.

3. Cover block with sheet moss and secure with floral U-pins.

Add Florals:

1. Insert two sponge mushrooms horizontally, placing them so they extend over the right front edge of the saucer. Insert other sponge mushroom on the back side of the wreath.

2. Insert stock, letting one extend horizontally from the left side of the wreath and placing one vertically on the opposite side of the wreath.

3. Insert and glue lilies, one slightly above the other, centered at the base of the wreath.

4. Fill in around the flowers on both sides with foliage.

5. Insert and glue hydrangea, snowball, and filler flowers around the lilies and stock on both sides of the wreath.

6. Glue a small cluster of greens and blossoms at the top right of the wreath. ❏

Design Variation

Wrap a metal ring with ivy and use it as a wreath base instead of a grapevine wreath.

Fresh Idea

Substitute fresh floral foam for plastic foam (Styrofoam®) in this design. Anchor a low dish that will hold water and use the same or different cut flowers as the artifical ones. Use sheet moss soaked in water to hide the foam if needed. Keep the foam in a pool of water to extend the life of the fresh flowers. Be sure damp moss is in the container or it will drip water on to the table top.

Fresh Wreaths

Nothing can beat the beauty of fresh greens and flowers fashioned into a wreath. Many people shy away from using fresh materials because they think it is too difficult and the results are not long-lasting. For this section, I designed two fresh wreaths that are easy to make *and* long-lasting: the salal wreath looks great fresh and will dry to a beautiful sage green; the classic evergreen wreath will last several weeks in a cool environment.

Pictured right: Salal Wreath. Instructions begin on page 92.

Salal Wreath

Salal - sometimes called "lemon leaf" - is a bright, shiny green leaf that's perfect for wreaths and available from most florists. Use fresh Salal for this wreath; it will dry naturally in to a lovely gray green. Make the wreath extra full if you want to keep it as a dried wreath as the leaves will shrink slightly.

Level of difficulty

Time to complete

SUPPLIES & TOOLS

Wire wreath frame, 14"

1 bunch salal (about 20 stems)

Dried pink roses

Natural raffia

Preserved ming fern

Chenille stem

Floral paddle wire

Floral tape

INSTRUCTIONS

Cover the Frame:

1. Cut salal stems into 6"-8" lengths.

2. At the 10 o'clock position on the wreath frame, place a couple of sprigs with the leaves, shiny side up. Using floral paddle wire, wrap wire around the stems and across all supports of the entire frame. (photo

1) Continue placing stems and binding to frame with wire, overlapping the leaves slightly.

Add Accents:

1. Arrange the dried roses in a fan shape. Bind the cluster with floral tape a few inches below the flowers.

2. Form the raffia into a multi-loop bow with 4" loops. Tie knots in the ends of each streamer and trim.

3. Use wire to attach the rose cluster at the 1 o'clock position on the wreath.

4. Glue ming fern around the rose cluster.

5. Glue raffia bow to roses. Weave some strands of raffia around the wreath.

6. Attach a chenille stem to top back as a hanger. ❏

Salal Facts

Salal is an evergreen that is common in southeast British Columbia. Its strong, flexible branches can withstand heavy snows because they bend rather than break.

Photo 1. Wrapping the wire around the stems and wreath frame.

Fresh Evergreen & Tulips Wreath

Fresh evergreen wreaths look beautiful and smell grand. This wreath, with accents of red silk tulips and red berries, celebrates the winter season and the promise of spring.

Level of difficulty ❀ ❀

Time to complete ⏰ ⏰ ⏰

SUPPLIES & TOOLS

Wire wreath frame, 16"

Fresh evergreens of choice

4 red silk tulips

3 red artificial berry stems

2 yds. red sheer ribbon, 1-1/2" wide

3 pinecones

Chenille stem

Floral paddle wire

Glue

Pruning shears

Photo 1. Cutting the evergreens with pruning shears.

Photo 2. Wiring together clusters of evergreen stems.

Photo 3. Attaching the tulips with wire.

Continued on page 96

Fresh Evergreen & Tulips Wreath

Continued from page 94

INSTRUCTIONS

Attach Greens:

1. Cut evergreens stems into 6" lengths. (photo 1)

2. Make clusters of stems, securing them with paddle wire. (photo 2)

3. Starting at the 2 o'clock position on the wreath frame, lay a cluster of evergreens on the frame. Wrap wire around the evergreens and wire frame tightly. Continue around the wreath, slightly overlapping the evergreen clusters and wiring them in place.

Add Accents:

1. Working one at a time, gently shape each tulip into an arc with your hands.

2. Lay tulips across top of wreath, shape as needed, and attach with wire. (photo 3)

3. Wire berry sprays around the tulips, letting them cascade down the right and left sides of the wreath.

4. Form red sheer ribbon into a two-loop bow with 3" loops and 18" streamers.

5. Glue and wire bow at the mid-point of the tulip stems.

6. Glue a cluster of pinecones around the bow.

7. Twist a chenille stem into a loop on the top back of the wreath as a hanger. ❏

Seasonal Wreaths

I marvel at the changing of the seasons and feel blessed with the inspirations of each new season - wreaths are a fun way to celebrate seasonal colors and beauty. For this section, I designed a collection of wreaths that are easy and fun to create. You can make them just as I did or use the wreaths as inspiration for creating you own seasonal beauties. If your wreath doesn't turn out exactly like mine, that's great - it is uniquely yours, just as each season is unique.

Pictured right: Autumn Harvest Wreath. Instructions begin on page 98.

Autumn Harvest Wreath

Bunches of grapes, crabapples, and orange berries make me think of a bountiful autumn harvest. This twiggy wreath is striking background that showcases the bright colors and textures of fall.

Level of difficulty

Time to complete

Photo 1. Securing the crabapple stem with wire.

Photo 2. Curving the spines of the feathers with the dull side of a knife.

SUPPLIES & TOOLS

Twig wreath, 15"

2 grape bunches

10 crabapples on a branch

Orange berries

4 pheasant feathers, 12"

Green filler seed sprays

2 green silk leaf stems

Reindeer moss

Chenille stem

Knife

Floral paddle wire

Glue gun and glue

INSTRUCTIONS

1. Twist a chenille stem into a loop on the top back of the wreath base as a hanger.

2. Wire grape clusters to the wreath at about 10 o'clock and 7 o'clock. (Don't use glue - glue does not hold to the grapes' slick surface very well.)

3. Insert and glue crabapple stems around the grape clusters, wedging the stems between the twigs of the base and securing them with wire. (photo 1) Shape the stems into curves for a natural look.

4. Insert and glue the orange berries at about 9 o'clock and 12 o'clock.

5. Pull the dull side of a knife along the spines of the pheasant feathers to curve them. (photo 2) Insert and glue three of the pheasant feathers diagonally across the wreath. Cut the other pheasant feather in half and insert at top of wreath.

6. Glue green seed sprays randomly among fruit.

7. Strip leaves from stems. Glue leaves randomly among fruit, tucking in base.

8. Coil the stems left from leaf spray and glue into wreath as shown in photo.

9. Glue reindeer moss to add texture and hide glue. ❏

Spring Pussy Willow Wreath

The emerging of pussy willow and forsythia in spring is always a time of anticipation. I am fascinated by the soft, fluffy catkins of pussy willow, and this wreath showcases them beautifully. Add a chirping bird with tiny eggs for this great-looking salute to spring.

Level of difficulty

Time to complete

SUPPLIES & TOOLS

8 artificial pussy willow stems, 24"

Forsythia

3 grape hyacinths

Purple pansy cluster

Yellow mushroom bird, 3"

Bird's nest with eggs, 2-1/2"

3 yds. pink plaid ribbon, 1-1/2" wide

Maidenhair fern

Floral wire *or* cable ties

Floral tape

Glue

Wood pick

INSTRUCTIONS

1. Twist the pussy willow into a loose circle about 12" in diameter, allowing some of the ends to hang free. Secure in place with floral wire or cable ties. Cover wires or ties with floral tape.

2. Form the pink plaid ribbon into a two-loop bow with 4" loops. Trim ends of ribbon in V-shapes. Wire and glue bow to about the 5 o'clock position.

3. Insert and glue a wood pick in the bottom of the bird's nest. Glue nest slightly above the bow.

4. Glue bird to back edge of nest.

5. Create a vertical cluster of grape hyacinths to the right of the nest.

6. Cut short lengths of forsythia and twist into the pussy willow as shown. Secure with floral wire.

7. Glue maidenhair fern around the bow.

8. Insert and glue pansy cluster around the nest. ❑

Fresh Idea

Fresh pussy willow can be substituted for the artificial ones. Choose stems that are pliable and easy to shape.

Forcing Forsythia

Near the end of winter everyone longs for fresh garden flowers. It is easy to have a bit of spring inside by forcing forsythia branches from your garden. Here's how:

1. *Choose and cut branches of forsythia near the top of the plant with closely spaced buds. (The larger the buds the quicker they will bloom.)*

2. *Re-cut stems at an angle and place in a vase of cool water for a couple of days. Remove any buds below the water line.*

3. *Re-cut again. Place stems in warm water in a bright location. In a week or so, you will have a bright golden bouquet.*

River's Edge Wreath

Image yourself at the river's edge - the cool water, the polished rocks sparkling in the sunshine, and the lush green plants along the bank. You can bring home that look and feel with a river's edge wreath. A sturdy wood base is the beginning - you can make your own from pressed fiberboard or plywood.

Level of difficulty

Time to complete

SUPPLIES & TOOLS

Wooden wreath base, 12" diameter with 6" center opening, 3" wide

Polished river rocks

Pea gravel

White sand-finish paint

2 sponge mushrooms

4 artificial mushrooms, 2" and 3" tall

Curly willow branch, 14" long

Assorted trailing foliage and ferns

Green reindeer moss

Other green moss

Glue made for mosaics or glass

Sandpaper

Cloth

Floral tape

Floral wire, medium weight

INSTRUCTIONS

Prepare the Base:
1. Sand the wooden wreath base to rough up the surface. (This helps the rocks adhere better.) Wipe away any sanding dust with a damp cloth.
2. Use floral tape to tape together three medium-weight floral wires. Twist the wires around the wreath and bring them to the back. Twist into a loop for hanging. Because the wreath is heavy, be sure the wire encircles the whole wreath base.

Add Rocks & Gravel:
Place wreath on a flat protected surface where you can leave it undisturbed while the glue dries.
1. Starting on the outside edge of the wreath, apply glue to the river rocks one at a time, following the glue manufacturer's instructions. Glue the rocks in random circles around the outside edges of the wreath.
2. Closer to the inside of the wreath, add pea gravel. Allow a 1" wide band around the inside opening of the wreath to remain uncovered. Allow to dry.
3. Fill in the spaces between the river rocks with pea gravel as needed.

Paint:
1. Working in a well-ventilated area and following the directions on the can, spray a circle of sand paint about 1" wide around the center opening of the wreath. It's okay if some paint spatters on the pea gravel. Allow to dry.
2. Wipe away any unwanted sand paint.

Add Accents:
Place wreath with hanger at the top back as you work.
1. Remove stems from sponge mushrooms. Glue horizontally one sponge mushroom at 1 o'clock and one at 7 o'clock.
2. Glue a curly willow branch diagonally between the sponge mushrooms.
3. Glue one 2" and one 3" artificial mushroom to the top of each sponge mushroom.
4. Glue some trailing foliage beneath each sponge mushroom, allowing foliage to cascade downward.
5. Fill in around the mushrooms with ferns and other greenery.
6. Glue clumps of green reindeer moss and other green moss to hide glue and add texture. ❏

Halloween Boo Bats Wreath

This haunting Halloween wreath includes bats and a big BOO. Creating this wreath is not scary, and it's hauntingly fun to display.

Level of difficulty

Time to complete

SUPPLIES & TOOLS

Plastic foam (Styrofoam®) disc, 12" diameter, 1" thick

Cardboard, 13" x 13"

Wood letters, 6" tall, 2 Bs and 4 Os

2 foam bat cutouts with 8" wingspans

2 yds. neon green sheer ribbon, 2-1/2" wide

6 orange mums

Birch twigs, 18" long

Orange berry sprays

Tradescantia vine

White string

4 white pearl-head pins

Chenille stem

Floral spray paints - yellow, black, orange

Floral U-pins

Floral wire

Pencil

Glue

Scissors *or* craft knife

INSTRUCTIONS

Prepare:

1. Place the disc on the cardboard and trace around it. Cut out the cardboard and glue to the foam disc. (This strengthens the Styrofoam and helps keep it from breaking.)
2. Insert and glue a chenille stem hanger on the back of the disc. Reinforce with U-pins.
3. In a well-ventilated area, following the package instructions, paint the disc with yellow floral spray paint, the twigs and one "BOO" with black, and the other "BOO" with orange. Paint with at least two coats; add more coats if the color is not as intense as you want. Allow to dry.
4. Using string, weave a spider web on top of one orange "O."
5. Glue orange "BOO" on top of black "BOO" slightly offsetting the letters, with the spider web "O" last.

Assemble:

1. Glue "BOO"s across the bottom of the disc.
2. Make a cluster of black twigs about 18" long. Bind together in the center with floral wire. With glue and floral U-pins, attach twigs to left side of disc.
3. Insert and glue berries among the twigs.
4. Using the photo as a guide, insert and glue the foliage from the Tradescantia vine to the left side of the wreath and beneath the last "O."
5. Insert and glue orange mums.
6. Cut an 18" length of ribbon. Use floral U-pins and glue to attach to the cluster of flowers below the "O." Weave the remainder of the ribbon through the twigs and flowers on the left side of the design and secure with glue. Trim ends of ribbon into V-shapes.
7. Glue bats to disc and letters as shown.
8. Insert and glue pearl pins to the bats for eyes. ❑

Winter Wonderland Wreath

Snowflakes, glistening silver accents, and frosted evergreens comprise this winter wreath. The white roses are a romantic, unexpected touch. Using purchased ornaments and an evergreen wreath as a base makes this wreath easy to complete.

Level of difficulty

Time to complete

SUPPLIES & TOOLS

Frosted tip evergreen wreath, 20"

4 yds. white open-weave (net-type) ribbon

3 white and crystal snowflakes, 10" wide

14 white open roses

Icy twigs

Silver foliage

Chenille stem

Glue gun and glue

INSTRUCTIONS

1. Fluff and shape evergreen wreath to achieve a full, lush look.

2. Twist a chenille stem around the top back of the wreath for a hanger.

3. Form white ribbon into a four-loop bow with 5" loops and 18" streamers. Glue bow to top center of wreath. Twist a couple of evergreen sprigs across center of the bow to secure further.

4. Using the photo as a guide for placing snowflakes, glue and attach using evergreen sprigs.

5. Glue the bow streamers behind the snowflakes. Trim ends of ribbon diagonally.

6. Insert and glue icy twigs around the bow.

7. Insert and glue silver foliage around the bow, letting the foliage cascade off the bottom right of the wreath.

8. Glue clusters of roses around the wreath, using the photo as a guide for placement. ❏

Designer's Tip

When working with evergreen wreaths and garlands made of wired artificial branches, try twisting a couple of the branches together to secure ornaments, bows, and other decorations rather than using wire or glue.

Sounds of Christmas Wreath

Jingle bells and sheet music scrolls embellish this classic gold and white evergreen wreath. It's a great addition to almost any holiday decorating theme. You can create the wreath in an evening, making it a perfect gift for yourself or a friend.

Level of difficulty

Time to complete

SUPPLIES & TOOLS

Artificial evergreen wreath, 20"

3 gold jingle bell clusters

10 assorted gold jingle bells

10 gold pinecones

Sheet music

3 yds. gold-and-white metallic plaid wire-edge ribbon, 3" wide

3 yds. gold sheer metallic wire-edge ribbon, 1-1/2"

Assorted leaves

Gold spray glitter

Chenille stem

Floral wire

Glue gun and glue

INSTRUCTIONS

Prepare:
1. Fluff and shape evergreen wreath to achieve a full, lush look.
2. Twist chenille stem around the top back of the wreath for a hanger.
3. Form the plaid ribbon into a four-loop bow with 5" loops and 20" streamers.
4. Form the gold ribbon into a four-loop bow with 3" loops and 18" streamers.

Assemble:
1. Glue plaid bow to top center of the wreath.
2. Glue gold bow centered on top of plaid bow.
3. Bend a couple of evergreen sprigs across the bows to hold them in place.
4. Weave the steamers down the right and left sides of the wreath, attaching them at about the mid-point on each side. Trim ends of ribbon into V-shapes.
5. Wire a jingle bell cluster at the mid-point on the right and left sides of the wreath and one at the center of the bow.
6. Roll the sheet music into three scrolls about 5" long. Secure with glue. Glue scrolls into bottom center of wreath.
7. Glue a cluster of three cones to the right of the music scrolls. Glue the remainder of the cones scattered around the wreath.
8. Glue assorted jingle bells on the wreath as desired.
9. Glue in leaves as needed for contrast and to add fullness.
10. Spray entire wreath with a light coat of gold spray glitter. Allow to dry before hanging. ❑

Fresh Idea

You can use a fresh evergreen wreath, one you make or one you purchase. The fresh scent of evergreens always smells clean and delightful. Snowflakes, and jingle bells can be either wired or glued in place.

Designer Tips

• *If you cannot find jingle bell clusters, you can make your own by stringing various sizes of bells on lengths of floral wire.*

• *Natural pinecones can be sprayed with gold floral paint.*

• *To keep the bow fresh-looking when storing, stuff each loop with tissue paper.*

Wreaths for Gifting

A handcrafted wreath is a thoughtful gift for almost any occasion, and all the wreaths in this book would make lovely gifts. In this section, I included a few wreaths designed especially for gift giving. Personalize any wreath with the recipient's name for a memorable gift.

Happy Birthday Jeff

Happy Birthday Celebration Wreath

Bring out the party horns and sweets! Two wire wreath forms are filled with sweet treats and trimmed with party horns and flowers. Use it for a birthday, New Year's, or any celebratory occasion. Use a computer to print out a message on colored paper.

Level of difficulty

Time to complete

Pictured left: Supplies for wreath.

Instructions begin on page 112.

SUPPLIES & TOOLS

2 wire box wreath frames, 12"

4 party horns

4 gerbera daisies in bright colors

2 yds. red metallic ribbon, 1" wide

12 oz. assorted wrapped candy bar miniatures

Red spray paint

Plastic foam block, 2" x 2"

Chenille stem

Glue gun and glue

Floral U-pins

Optional: Birthday sign, 8-1/2" X 11" and wide clear tape

INSTRUCTIONS

1. In a well-ventilated area, following the manufacturer's instructions, spray wreath frames with red paint. Allow to dry. Repeat.

2. Place one wreath frame with the curved side up. Wire and glue two party horns at 1 o'clock and 10 o'clock.

3. Cut plastic foam block in half. Glue and pin half to the left of the top horns (photo 1) and the other half below the bottom horns.

4. Insert and glue one daisy in the bottom half-block and three daisies in the top half-block. (photo 2)

5. Cut ribbon into 1-yard lengths. Form each piece into a two-loop bow with 3" loops. Glue one bow to the top cluster and the other to the bottom cluster.

6. Place the other wreath frame so the curved side is down. Fill with candy. Place the decorated wreath frame on top of the candy-filled wreath frame. Use short lengths of wire to attach the two together, placing the wires so they can't be seen.

7. Twist a chenille stem to top back to make a hanger loop.

8. *Optional:* Place wreath on printed sign and trace around wreath. Cut out circle shape and tape to back of wreath. ❑

Photo 1. Gluing the top two horns.

Photo 2. Adding the three daisies to the foam block.

Spa Retreat Basket Wreath

Creating a wreath around the edge of a basket or other container is a fun twist. This spa retreat basket is filled with soaps, lotions and pampering goodies and surrounded by a wreath of flowers and grasses.

Level of difficulty

Time to complete

SUPPLIES & TOOLS

Round low basket

Spa items to fill basket

Hydrangea blossoms - pink, purple, green

Assorted ferns, ivy, or other foliage

Bear grass

1-1/2 yds. sheer lavender ribbon, 1" wide

2 yds. purple eyelash yarn

Floral wire

Floral tape

Glue

INSTRUCTIONS

1. Cut greenery into short sprigs. Wire and glue greens around the rim of the basket, allowing the greenery to flow over the outside edge of the basket.

2. Cut hydrangea blossoms into small clusters. Glue clusters of alternating colors around the rim of the basket.

3. Cut twelve blades of bear grass about 12" long. Divide into three bunches. Tape each end of each bunch together with floral tape.

4. Insert and glue both ends of one bunch of grass so the grass arcs above the flowers. Repeat to make a total of three arcs.

5. Weave and glue eyclash yarn through the flowers and greens.

6. Cut lavender ribbon into three 18" lengths. Form each length into three loops. Glue ribbon loops to the wreath.

7. Fill the basket with the goodies. ❑

Baby Gift Wreath

A teddy bear sits snuggled in a wreath wrapped in fleece; below hangs a basket filled with baby necessities. This would be a great gift for Mother and new baby. It could also be the centerpiece for a baby shower. When giving, place your gift in the basket. Later, the wreath can be placed on a door and filled with toys, a potted plant, or flowers.

Level of difficulty

Time to complete

SUPPLIES & TOOLS

Plastic foam (Styrofoam®) wreath base, 12" x 2"

1 yd. fleece, 36" wide - color of your choice

White wall basket, 10" wide, 7" tall

Teddy bear, 9" tall

5 gerbera daisies - 3 hot pink, 2 purple

Pink seed spray

Assorted foliage

Baby gifts

Acrylic craft paint - Blue

Chenille stems

Small artist's brush

Scissors

Floral U-pins

Glue

INSTRUCTIONS

1. Using the small brush, paint the rim of the basket with two coats of blue paint. Allow to dry.

2. Place fleece right side down. Place the wreath base about 2" from one edge. Cut out a rough circle about 2" wider than the wreath base. Cut an X in the center of the fleece circle.

3. Pin and glue fleece to the back of the wreath. Cut small slits around the center of the wreath. Turn and pin the fleece to the back.

4. Attach basket to bottom of wreath with chenille stems.

5. Glue the bear at the center bottom of the wreath.

6. Glue a spray of foliage at 10 o'clock and 4 o'clock.

7. Insert and glue one hot pink and one purple daisy to each foliage spray.

8. Glue pink seed sprays around each daisy.

9. Glue a cluster of foliage, a hot pink daisy, and some pink seed sprays at the front lower left of basket.

10. Fill the basket with goodies and place a toy around the bear's arm.

11. Twist a chenille stem. Insert and glue at the top back of the wreath for a hanger. Reinforce hanger with floral U pins. ❑

Fresh Idea

Instead of using silk flowers consider adding a bud vase of fresh greens and blossoms. This would be a great gift to deliver to the new mom and baby in the hospital.

Wedding Wreath

Open ivory roses surround a heart studded with tiny ivory stephanotis blossoms. Wouldn't this wreath look wonderful displayed near the guest book or on a door? You could add the couple's names to the wreath for a personalized touch.

Level of difficulty

Time to complete

SUPPLIES & TOOLS

Plastic foam (Styrofoam®) disc, 10" diameter, 1" thick

Plastic foam (Styrofoam®) heart, 5" x 1"

12 open ivory roses with leaves

Flat leaves

Variegated ivy

50 or more ivory stephanotis blossoms

Chenille stem

Wire cutters

Glue

INSTRUCTIONS

1. Trim stems of ivory roses to about 1". Cut foliage from the roses.

2. Insert and glue the roses at a slight angle outward around the edge of the foam disc.

3. Insert and glue the rose leaves outward beneath the roses.

4. Remove plastic veins, if any, from the flat leaves. Glue to cover the center of the disc.

5. Glue a row of variegated ivy leaves pointing outward around the edge of the foam heart.

6. Remove the stephanotis blooms from their stems. Glue them one at a time to cover the top of the heart.

7. Glue heart at center of disc.

8. Twist chenille stem into a loop. Insert and glue to top back of disc as a hanger. ❏

Stephanotis Facts

Stephanotis, a member of the milkweed family, is native to Madagascar. The plant is a woody twining vine with dark green waxy leaves that produces fragrant, white star-shaped blossoms that are sometimes called the wedding flower.

For The Birds Wreath

This wreath not only looks great - displayed outdoors, it will be a treat for the birds. They'll eat the corn and millet, and the raffia and Spanish moss provide tempting fiber to be added to a nest.

Level of difficulty

Time to complete

SUPPLIES & TOOLS

Wire frame, 15"

12 ears Indian corn on the cob

Millet

Wheat

Green and natural raffia

Spanish moss

Chenille stem

Cable ties, 8"

Floral wire

Glue

INSTRUCTIONS

1. Remove the shucks from the Indian corn.

2. Place the wire wreath frame with the open side up. Starting with the largest ears of corn, place corn on wreath frame and secure with a cable tie. Continue around the wreath securing the ears of corn with cable ties.

3. Tie natural raffia across each cable tie to hide it.

4. Glue in millet and wheat between the ears of corn.

5. Form a green raffia multi-loop bow with 4" loops and 12" streamers. Wire and glue bow to wreath. Glue some millet to middle of bow.

6. Fill in with Spanish moss as needed.

7. Twist a chenille stem on the top back as a hanger. ❏

Wine Bottle Wreath

Wine is a lovely hostess gift; make the bottle even more beautiful with a tiny wreath.

Level of difficulty

Time to complete

SUPPLIES & TOOLS

Grapevine wreath, 3"
Small red grape bunch
Natural raffia
Natural color tiny blossoms and foliage
2 yds. 24 gauge brass wire
Pencil
Floral wire
Wire cutters
Scissors
Glue gun and glue

INSTRUCTIONS

1. Wire grape cluster to left side of wreath.

2. Cut two 1-yard lengths of brass wire. Coil around a pencil to form tendrils. Remove wire from pencil, uncoil a little, and twist in the grape bunch.

3. Form the raffia into a multi-loop bow with 2" loops and 4" streamers. Glue to top of grape bunch. Knot ends of streamers and trim.

4. Glue some foliage and natural color blossoms in the center of the raffia bow.

5. Place wreath on wine bottle neck. ❏

Functional Wreaths

How about crafting a wreath that keeps track of time? Or one that holds memos or feeds the birds? The following wreaths are fun to make and to view. Create one for yourself or as a gift.

Nut Candle Wreath

The natural colors and textures of nuts and pods decorate this wreath with a decidedly masculine flair.

SUPPLIES & TOOLS

Plastic foam (Styrofoam®) wreath base, 6" diameter, 1" thick

Assorted nuts and tiny pods

Reindeer moss

Pillar candle, 3" x 7"

Knife

Brown floral tape

Glue gun and glue

Level of difficulty

Time to complete

INSTRUCTIONS

1. If your wreath doesn't have a rounded edge, use a knife to bevel the outside edge of the wreath base. Brush away any loose particles.

2. Wrap wreath completely in brown floral tape. This hides the foam and gives a nice surface for gluing. (photo 1)

3. Starting at the lower outside edge, glue nuts and pods around the top and outside edge of the wreath base until the wreath base is covered - but do **not** glue nuts to the inside edge. (photo 2)

4. Place the candle in the wreath opening and make adjustments to the nuts as needed so the candle fits. Remove candle.

5. Glue tiny bits of green reindeer moss to fill spaces between the nuts and hide visible glue.

6. Place candle in center of the wreath. **Caution:** NEVER leave a burning candle unattended. ❏

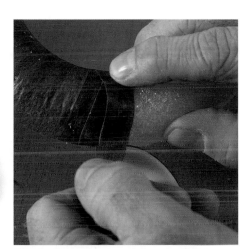

Photo 1. Wrapping the wreath base with brown floral tape.

Photo 2. Gluing the nuts on the wrapped wreath base.

Clock Wreath

Who could resist checking the time, especially when the clock is
surrounded with a wreath? Make this wreath as shown or
substitute flowers and ribbons that coordinate with your decor.
Is it time for a clock wreath at your house?

Level of difficulty ❀

Time to complete ⏰ ⏰

SUPPLIES & TOOLS

Round clock, 8" diameter

Grapevine wreath, 12" diameter

Green snowball (form flower)

Blue hydrangea (form flower)

Raspberries

3 yds. lime green ribbon, 1-1/2" wide

Fern fronds

Bear grass

Acrylic craft paint - Green

Small artist's brush

Floral tape

Glue gun and glue

Scissors

Photo 1. Gluing the reindeer moss on the clock frame.

INSTRUCTIONS

Prepare:

1. Using the small brush, paint the clock frame with green acrylic paint. Allow to dry. Repeat. (This helps blend the clock into wreath.)
2. Wedge clock in center of grapevine wreath. (If the opening is too small, trim away some vines.) *Option:* Glue clock to wreath.
3. Glue clumps of green reindeer moss around edge of clock face. (photo 1)
4. Cut an 18" length of ribbon. Set aside.
5. Form remaining ribbon into a two-loop bow with 3" loops and 10" streamers.

Assemble:

1. Weave 18" length of ribbon into right side of wreath. Glue bow at 10 o'clock. Trim ends of ribbons into V-shapes.
2. Glue snowball clusters at 11 o'clock, 1 o'clock, 5 o'clock, and 9 o'clock.
3. Glue hydrangea blossoms into each snowball cluster.
4. Glue raspberries in place.
5. Glue fern fronds around outside edge of the wreath.
6. Cluster four to six blades of bear grass. Floral tape each end. Make a total of four.
7. Glue bear grass in arcs around the center of the wreath.
8. Twist a chenille stem into a loop on the top back of the wreath for a hanger. ❏

Kitchen Memo Board Wreath

What a great kitchen shower gift! This wreath is both fun and functional. A metal pizza pan becomes a memo board; magnets are glued to the backs of crabapples. Be sure the pizza pan is NOT aluminum; if it is, the magnets will not stick.

Level of difficulty

Time to complete

SUPPLIES & TOOLS

Metal pizza pan, 12" diameter

Small wood rolling pin, 12" long

2 wooden spoons

Yellow zinnias with 2 blooms and 2 buds

Yellow-gold berry sprays

2 yellow crabapples

2 yds. butterscotch print ribbon, 1-1/2" wide

Assorted greenery

Yellow filler flowers

Chenille stems

2 round magnets, 3/4"

Hammer and nail

Glue gun and glue

Craft knife

INSTRUCTIONS

1. Use the hammer and nail to puncture a hole at the top of the pizza pan. Insert a chenille stem in the hole and twist on the back to form a hanger.

2. Position rolling pin on pan. With a pencil, mark the pan where the rolling pin touches the rim. Set rolling pin aside and puncture the pan with hammer and nail at the two marked places. Replace rolling pin. Twist chenille stems around rolling pin handles and through the holes. Twist tightly to secure.

3. Puncture a hole on the opposite side of the pan. Twist a chenille stem around the wooden spoons and attach them to the pan.

4. Form the ribbon into a two-loop bow with 3" loops and 12" streamers. Glue bow at center of spoons. Trim ends of streamers into V-shapes.

5. Glue one yellow zinnia blossom to top right of rolling pin. Glue other zinnia to middle of bow. Glue buds extending above and to the right of the bow.

6. Fill in around the spoons and rolling pin with greenery, followed by berries and yellow filler flowers.

7. Cut a slice from one side of each crabapple so it lies flat and will not roll. Glue a magnet to the flat place on each crabapple. Place on the pan. ❑

Christmas Candle & Candy Wreaths

With just a few materials you can create these candle rings with candies quickly and easily. They would be great gifts for friends, co-workers, or your children's teachers.

Level of difficulty

Time to complete

SUPPLIES & TOOLS

For votive candle and candy:

Rose style clay pot, 3"

Clay saucer, 6-3/4"

Glass votive cup and candle

Ivory candle

For pillar candle and candy:

Clay pot, 5"

Clay saucer, 8-1/4"

Ivory pillar candle, 3" diameter, 12" tall

For both:

Red spray paint

1-1/2 yds. red plaid ribbon, 1-1/2" wide

Evergreen sprigs or picks

Jingle bells

Red berries

Crabapples

Assorted miniature ornaments - your choice

Wrapped red and white mints

Glue

INSTRUCTIONS

1. Glue pots upside down in the centers of their saucers.
2. In a well-ventilated area, following the manufacturer's instructions, spray pots and saucers with two coats of red. Allow to dry.
3. Twist evergreens together to form a circle slightly larger than the small end of each pot and adjust so the evergreen wreaths stay around the pot.
4. Form a bow from plaid ribbon in scale with each wreath. Glue bows in place. Trim ends of ribbons in V-shapes.
5. Make loops of ribbon and glue around each wreath.
6. Using the photo as guide, glue jingle bells, berries, crabapples, and ornaments to wreaths.
7. Place votive cup with candle on smaller pot. Place pillar on top of larger pot. Fill saucers with mints. ❏

Metric Conversion Chart

Inches to Millimeters and Centimeters

Inches	MM	CM
1/8	3	.3
1/4	6	.6
3/8	10	1.0
1/2	13	1.3
5/8	16	1.6
3/4	19	1.9
7/8	22	2.2
1	25	2.5
1-1/4	32	3.2
1-1/2	38	3.8
1-3/4	44	4.4
2	51	5.1
3	76	7.6
4	102	10.2
5	127	12.7
6	152	15.2
7	178	17.8
8	203	20.3
9	229	22.9
10	254	25.4
11	279	27.9
12	305	30.5

Yards to Meters

Yards	Meters	Yards	Meters
1/8	.11	2	1.83
1/4	.23	3	2.74
3/8	.34	4	3.66
1/2	.46	5	4.57
5/8	.57	6	5.49
3/4	.69	7	6.40
7/8	.80	8	7.32
1	.91	9	8.23
		10	9.14

Index